D1443856

HANNIBAL

Great General of the Ancient World

Karen Clemens Warrick

Enslow Publishers, Inc.

40 Industrial Road   PO Box 38
Box 398   Aldershot
Berkeley Heights, NJ 07922   Hants GU12 6BP
USA   UK

http://www.enslow.com

Library of Congress Cataloging-in-Publication Data

Warrick, Karen Clemens.
    Hannibal : great general of the ancient world / by Karen Clemens Warrick.— 1st. ed.
       p. cm. — (Rulers of the ancient world)
    Includes bibliographical references and index.
    ISBN 0-7660-2564-0
    1. Hannibal, 247–182 B.C.—Juvenile literature. 2. Generals—Tunisia—Carthage (Extinct
city)—Biography—Juvenile literature. 3. Punic War, 2nd, 218–201 B.C.—Juvenile literature.
[1. Carthage (Extinct city)—History—Juvenile literature. 2. Rome—History—Republic,
265–30 B.C.—Juvenile literature.] I. Title. II. Series.
    DG249.W37 2006
    937'.04'092—dc22

                                           2005007332

Printed in the United States of America

10 9 8 7 6 5 4 3 2 1

To Our Readers:
We have done our best to make sure that all Internet Addresses in this book were active and
appropriate when we went to press. However, the author and publisher have no control over and
assume no liability for the material available on those Internet sites or on other Web sites they may
link to. Any comments or suggestions can be sent by e-mail to comments@enslow.com or to the
address on the back cover.

Illustration Credits: Alínari/Art Resource, NY, p. 1; ©The British Museum/Topham-HIP/The
Image Works, p. 100; Clipart.com, p. 66; © Corel Corporation, pp. 51, 139; Enslow Publishers, Inc.,
pp. 18, 76; © Mary Evans Picture Library/The Image Works, pp. 22, 82, 121; Paul Lunde/Saudi
Aramco World/PADIA, top of pp. 5, 15, 26, 36, 44, 52, 62, 72, 80, 89, 97, 106, 113, 123, 132;
Reproduced from the Collections of the Library of Congress, pp. 6, 12, 54, 59.

Cover Illustration: Alínari/Art Resource, NY

CONTENTS

ACROSS
THE ALPS

The army of Carthage, in North Africa, was on the move. It snaked across the plains of Gaul (present-day France) in 218 B.C. About fifty thousand foot soldiers marched through what is now southern France. Nearly nine thousand cavalry and forty elephants followed after them.[1] Their target was Rome in Italy. For almost fifty years, Carthage and Rome had been fighting over territory. They both wanted to control lands near the middle and western Mediterranean Sea.

The Carthaginian army moved east. Soldiers studied the mountains blocking their route. Italy was divided from the rest of Europe by the Alps. These craggy peaks seemed to protect the country from invasion. Most of the African soldiers had never seen such an enormous range of mountains.

General Hannibal Barca led the army. He planned to march foot soldiers, cavalry, and elephants across the Alps and attack Rome. He knew his enemy believed this was impossible. He planned to prove them wrong.[2]

Hannibal's army had reached the foothills. So far, tribes that claimed lands near the mountains had not

Hannibal, Great General of Carthage

attacked. Now the soldiers faced a new enemy—the rugged Italian Alps. Snow-covered peaks towered high above them. Few plants grew in the rocky soil. Crude huts clung to the steep hillsides. Even the local people looked fierce and rugged.

ATTACKED BY WILD MEN OF THE MOUNTAIN

Hannibal's army climbed the foothills of the Alps toward a low pass. Tribesmen appeared on the cliffs above. From that position, they could ambush his force. Hannibal ordered a halt and prepared to camp for the night. Scouts went ahead to gather information. They learned

THE AFRICAN CITY-STATE OF CARTHAGE

In 800 B.C., Phoenicians from Asia Minor settled Carthage. A queen named Elissa led the group.[3] They built a city on Africa's north coast, in modern-day Tunisia. It was located on the Mediterranean Sea, opposite the island of Sicily.

Carthage had two excellent harbors and it grew into an important trading city. Its citizens were skillful boat builders and sailors. Merchants traded metals, ivory, pottery, jewelry, glassware, fruits, nuts, and wild animals. The people grew powerful and wealthy. Phoenicians also settled on Sicily, an island they shared with Greek colonists. This made it possible to control shipping in the Mediterranean.

In 500 B.C., the Persians conquered Phoenicia. They controlled the Aegean and eastern Mediterranean seas. Carthage was west of that territory and Persia gave the city-state its independence. Soon Carthage ruled North Africa, southern Sicily, and much of Spain.

By 300 B.C., Carthage and Greece battled over territories around the Mediterranean Sea. Carthage defeated the Greeks at sea. Rome defeated them in Italy.

Thirty-six years later, Carthage had a new enemy to face—Rome. Both wanted to control the seas. The Romans defeated Carthage during the First Punic War. The African city-state lost Sicily and control of the Mediterranean. Carthage was also forced to pay war damages to Rome. The peace treaty's terms were harsh. This angered the citizens of Carthage.[4] Rome became their greatest enemy.

the pass was guarded only during the daytime. The mountain men went home at night.

The next evening, the tribesmen returned to their village. Hannibal led a small band of soldiers up the narrow path. At dawn, the mountain men were surprised. They found Carthaginian troops standing guard on their cliffs. Meanwhile, the rest of Hannibal's great army packed up their gear and filed up the trail through the pass.

For a while the tribesmen watched the soldiers and pack animals. Then they attacked. Sure-footed, they swarmed down the steep slopes. This was their territory. They knew it well. The army from Carthage was not so lucky. They now had two enemies to deal with: the tribesmen and the unfamiliar mountain terrain. The army stretched out along the narrow track. Cliffs lined both sides of the trail. It was a difficult place to stand and fight. Many soldiers lost their footing and fell thousands of feet to their deaths. The attack frightened the horses and pack animals. They reared and lunged. Many animals loaded with packs and gear tumbled over the cliffs.

Hannibal saw that his men needed help. He charged down the slope and drove the tribesmen off. After order was restored, Hannibal and his men captured their village.[5] He wanted to teach the mountain men a lesson. He also seized enough cattle and grain to feed his army for three days. This show of force discouraged more attacks by the mountain tribe. For the next three days, Hannibal and his army moved on through the Alps with no problems.

WHY CROSS THE ALPS?

Hannibal was determined to attack Rome. He would have preferred to invade by sea, but that was not possible. Even if Carthage could have gathered a fleet large enough to move his army, the Romans controlled the sea. Hannibal would most likely have been attacked during his voyage. He did not want to risk a major defeat at sea.

The general's only way into Italy was over the Alps. Though it was risky, it did offer one advantage. Hannibal could barter or seize food and supplies from the mountain tribes. Historians today are certain he crossed the Alps. The exact route followed is not known. Possible routes have been studied and debated, but they are only educated guesses.

AMBUSHED!

Hannibal soon reached another tribe's territory. Village elders greeted him. They offered their friendship. The elders did not want to fight. They had heard how the general had punished the mountain men in the foothills below. The elders agreed to follow Hannibal's orders. They offered to supply guides and food for the army. They even gave him hostages to prove they meant what they said.

The general accepted the elders' offer, but did not trust them completely.[6] He took precautions as he lined up his troops. He placed the cavalry and elephants in front. Elephants were a defense against attack. The mountain men had not seen such creatures before. They feared the elephants and stayed away from them.[7]

Hannibal brought up the rear with his best warriors. He kept his eyes open. He watched for an ambush. For two days the army climbed steadily up into the Alps. They had no problems until they started across a difficult, narrow pass. Then more than one hundred fifty tribesmen attacked from the rear. Fortunately, Hannibal's cavalry and baggage train had already crossed the pass. These units would have been defenseless on such dangerous terrain.

The tribesmen split the Carthaginian army in two. Hannibal was cut off from the main body of his army. The men fighting with him drove the tribesmen off the pass. Some mountain men continued the fight. They rolled heavy boulders down onto the narrow path. The rocks crushed soldiers and animals. Finally, the tribesmen gave up and went home. The Carthaginians had won, but the skirmish had been costly. Many soldiers and pack animals lay dead by the side of the trail.

This was the last battle Hannibal fought during his passage over the Alps. Now the mountains became the real enemy. Snow began to fall. The trail grew wet and slippery. Men and animals struggled up steep slopes, climbing higher and higher. Soldiers who slipped plunged downward, clutching at anything that would break their slide. They often had to crawl on hands and knees to regain lost ground.

Hannibal's army reached the summit after nine days. He ordered a two-day halt. His men needed rest after the exhausting climb.[8] Most of the trek had been

HANNIBAL'S HISTORY

Much that is known of Hannibal's life is open to debate. Little information survived over the years. And that little bit must be questioned. Are the reports accurate? Are they a true record of history? Ancient historians wrote to entertain. They tried to tell a good story. They also wanted to teach lessons in loyalty to one's country.

Still, modern historians must rely on volumes written by these ancient historians. For example, the Roman Livy and the Greek Polybius, recorded Hannibal's story. The information was written down long after the general's death. It has been translated from ancient to modern languages. It has been studied and interpreted. Many modern books have been written about the Carthaginian general. Even today, however, it is impossible for anyone to know exactly what happened long ago when Hannibal crossed the Alps.

over mountainsides that had no obvious trails. Often the troops had to backtrack when the route became impassable. Sometimes guides from local tribes deliberately led them in the wrong direction. Little food was left. Men and animals were in danger of starving to death. It was November. Temperatures dropped below freezing at night. But at least the summit had been reached.

INTO ITALY

The descent into northern Italy through the Alps was shorter, but steeper. It soon became clear that going down would be more difficult than climbing to the summit. The track was covered with snow and ice. It was steep and slippery. It was almost impossible for the men to walk. The trail was especially hard for the animals. They stumbled and fell. There was constant chaos as men and beasts stumbled and slipped into and over each other on the narrow mountain passes.

The soldiers grew tired and discouraged.[9] Hannibal looked for a spot that offered a great view of the country below. Then he called his men together. The ancient historian Livy suggests that the general may have made the following speech: "My men," he said, "you are at this moment passing the protective barrier of Italy—nay more, you are walking over the very walls of Rome. . . . all will be easy going—no more hills to climb. After a

Before his army's dangerous descent from the Alps, Hannibal gave an inspiring speech to his men.

fight or two you will have the capital of Italy, the citadel [fortress] of Rome, in the hollow of your hands."[10]

Unfortunately, there were still huge obstacles left to overcome before Rome was in sight. Hannibal's army soon found itself on the edge of a steep, narrow cliff. Even a lightly-armed soldier could not get down by clinging to bushes and stumps. A detour had to be found. The army came to a halt. A space was leveled to make camp on the high ridge. They were trapped in that spot for four days. Little vegetation grew that high in the mountains and the pack animals nearly starved to death. Finally, Hannibal's scouts found another way.

As the army worked its way down the slopes, the struggle continued. At every turn they faced obstacles. A landslide blocked their route at one point. Debris covered the trail for several hundred yards.[11] Steep slopes made it impossible for the animals to go around.

HANNIBAL'S ELEPHANTS

Hannibal took about forty elephants on his trek across the Alps. There is no record of any of them dying during those fifteen days. Livy, the Roman historian, is the best source of information. Livy lists men, horses, and pack animals lost. He says nothing of elephants that died.

The Carthaginian general may have come down out of the snow-covered mountains with all his elephants.[12] No one knows for sure. It is certain that some did survive because Hannibal used them in battle during his first year in Italy.

Hannibal ordered his men to rebuild the path. It took one day to clear a track wide enough for the horse and mule train. It took three more days to make the trail wide enough so elephants could cross.[13]

Livy, the Roman historian, tells how Hannibal dealt with another obstacle. Boulders too large to move sometimes blocked his route. The general piled wood around the rocks. The wood was set on fire and kept burning until the surface of the boulders grew extremely hot. Then soldiers poured sour wine on the boulders. When the cooler liquid hit the hot rocks, the boulders cracked.[14] After the rocks cooled, men moved the broken pieces off the track.

Finally, Hannibal and his army reached the foothills. Here they found fields, valleys, and woods. The animals were put out to pasture. The troops rested for three days. They needed to recover from their journey.

The crossing of the Alps took fifteen days. During that time, Hannibal lost many men and animals. One prisoner later reported the losses. He claimed that Hannibal said thirty-six thousand men and a huge number of horses and pack animals died during this trek.[15]

Even with all these losses, Hannibal had accomplished what he had set out to do. He had marched a huge army of foot soldiers, cavalry, and elephants over the Alps. He entered Italy by a route considered impassable by such a large force. Now, the Carthaginian general was ready to launch his plan designed to bring Rome to its knees.

HANNIBAL'S EARLY YEARS

Hannibal Barca was born in 247 B.C. Legend says his birthplace was the small Mediterranean island of Malta. It is more likely he was born in Carthage.[1] He had three younger brothers: Hasdrubal, Hanno, and Mago. Their father, Hamilcar Barca, was a general in the Carthaginian army. He called his four sons "the Lion's Brood." He expected them to be great warriors when they grew up.

Carthage was then the most important city in North Africa. It sat on a peninsula; its shores were lined with sandy beaches. A hill towered near the peninsula's neck, blocking the route to the mainland. The hill made Carthage seem almost like an island. Sometimes north winds from the Mediterranean cooled the city. Other times, hot dry winds blew in from the south off the great Sahara desert.

The Barca family lived in a palace in the heart of the city. Their home was surrounded by other palaces and by temples built for the gods. Merchants and workmen lived elsewhere. Their homes were tall buildings similar in size to the apartment houses of today. There were also many warehouses, where goods to be traded were stored.

The city Hannibal called home was a great market. As a child, he was familiar with imports from around the ancient world. He knew that gold came from Africa, and silver and tin from Spain. He recognized the skins of deer, lions, and leopards, as well as elephant tusks and hides. His family bought Greek pottery and perfumes from the east. As the oldest son of one of the most important men in the city, Hannibal Barca was proud of Carthage.[2]

FIRST PUNIC WAR

When Hannibal was born, Carthage and Rome were at war. Hannibal's father took charge of the Carthaginian Army that year. Hamilcar, whose name means lightning or perhaps sword flash, sailed for Sicily.[3] He was assigned to defend a Carthaginian outpost with a protected harbor on the island's northwest corner. It was a good place for Carthaginian merchant ships and warships to make repairs. Timber and other raw materials were available. Carthage needed this outpost to protect shipping routes in the Mediterranean Sea.

Hamilcar landed in Sicily late in the war and took charge. Carthaginian troops held only a small corner of the island. He set up camp on a hilltop overlooking the

Why Carthage and Rome Went to War

When Rome was first founded, the city was on friendly terms with Carthage. At that time, the Romans made their living by farming. They only wanted land in Italy. They had no interest in controlling the Mediterranean Sea. Carthage was the sea power, with trading and war the most important occupations. During these early days, Rome and Carthage worked together.

In 320 B.C., Rome conquered the Greek cities in Italy. The Greeks were great sailors and traders, and they competed with Carthage for trade routes and markets. Once Rome controlled these Greek cities, they took over the Greek trade routes, which the Roman fleet was expected to protect.

Then, in 264 B.C., a dispute broke out among citizens of Messina, a town on Sicily. One side asked Carthage for help. The other side turned to Rome. When the Carthaginian fleet arrived in Messina's port, Rome sent troops. They forced the North African fleet to withdraw.

Carthage sent a larger fleet to drive the Romans from Messina. So Rome sent an army. They easily beat the Carthaginian force. The African city-state sent fifty thousand more soldiers to defend their claim to the island. More troops arrived from Italy, and Rome soon controlled most of Sicily.

This conflict was called the First Punic War. It lasted for more than twenty years.

harbor. The general protected his position there for three years. He kept the Roman legions from pushing his troops off Sicily, but did not win any important victories.

In 244 B.C., Hamilcar tried a new plan of attack. Under cover of darkness, he sailed for Drepana. This village was located on the northwest end of the island of Sicily. The town had been captured four years earlier by Romans. They had built a fort on a nearby mountain top. Hamilcar captured the town with his surprise attack. However, the war dragged on for three more years.

At the beginning of the First Punic War, the Carthaginian galleys, or warships, easily defeated their enemy in battles at sea. Then the Romans captured a Carthaginian ship. They used it as a model and built a

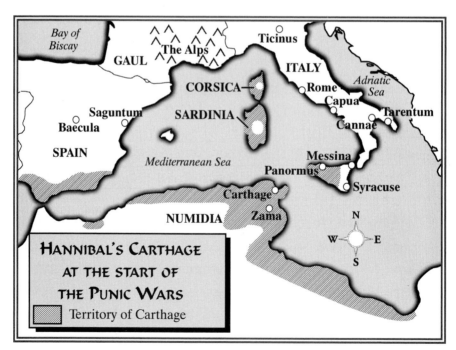

The Carthaginian Empire had spread throughout the Mediterranean before the start of the Punic Wars.

fleet of 120 galleys. Roman sailors also developed a new battle tactic. They armed warships with a long gangplank. A spike was attached to one end of the plank. During battle, Romans sailed close to an enemy ship and dropped the spiked end of the plank into its deck. The sharp spike secured the ships together and Romans used the gangplank to board the enemy vessel. This tactic helped the Roman navy defeat Carthage.[4]

In March 241 B.C., the Roman and Carthaginian fleets fought a battle near the coast of Sicily. It was a disastrous defeat for the African city-state. The Romans sank fifty of the fleet's ships and captured seventy more. The Romans took one hundred thousand prisoners. Carthaginian ships that could still sail retreated.[5] This battle ended the First Punic War.

Carthage was forced to agree to all of Rome's demands. Rome claimed all of Sicily. Carthaginian ships could not sail in waters off the coast of Italy. They could not attack Rome or any of Rome's allies, even to protect

HUNDREDS OF GALLEYS AND THOUSANDS OF SAILORS

During the First Punic War, Carthage and Rome built large fleets. A fleet might have as many as three hundred oared warships, called galleys. More than one hundred thousand sailors were needed to power these large fleets. Both cities used up most of their resources to build hundreds of warships and to pay, equip, and feed thousands of sailors.[6]

themselves. All Roman prisoners of war had to be surrendered and Carthage could not collect a ransom for them, which was a tradition of the time.

Carthage also was forced to pay Rome 3,200 talents over the next ten years. (A talent was a unit of money used by many ancient civilizations.) Roman citizens thought the peace terms were too lenient. The citizens of Carthage resented their harsh and unfair treatment.

Resentment grew over the next three years. Romans changed the terms of the peace agreement whenever they pleased.[7] They seized Sardinia from Carthage. The island was a stop on the city-state's trade routes. This seizure violated the treaty of 241 B.C.

Carthage tried to reclaim Sardinia. Rome drove them back across the Mediterranean Sea. They blamed the Africans for breaking the peace. Carthage had to pay more talents to Rome. They could not fight back against the stronger Roman navy.[8]

WAR IN SPAIN

In 237 B.C., Hamilcar again prepared for war. He planned to take his army to Spain, where Carthage already had settlements. The general wanted to expand into new territories. Spain had raw materials and Carthage could use these resources. It would help make the city-state rich again. Hamilcar also planned to recruit Spaniards for his army. He wanted to build a powerful fighting force. Since Spain was far from Italy, Rome should not have felt threatened by his plan. He expected to build his army and expand into new territory without interference.

The loss of Sicily to Rome had brought shame to the whole Barca family. Hamilcar was a proud man. He believed the island had been surrendered too easily. The defeat was a blow to his pride. He was determined to even the score. Some historians think Hamilcar had another goal in mind when he sailed for Spain. They believe he actually planned to invade Italy.[9]

Nine-year-old Hannibal begged to go with his father and Hamilcar agreed to take him. According to the Roman historian Livy, before sailing, the general made a sacrifice to the gods. He asked the gods to bless his venture. He then placed his son's hand on the sacrificed animal. He asked Hannibal to take a pledge, vowing never to forget that Rome was the deadly enemy of Carthage. Hannibal's three younger brothers all honored this pledge as well.[10]

HANNIBAL, THE YOUNG SOLDIER

In Spain, the nine-year-old Hannibal adapted to life in the army. He did not ask for special favors. Though his father was the commander-in-chief, Hannibal preferred to be treated like any young warrior. He dressed in a simple uniform. He spent hours cleaning and caring for his weapons and equipment. As the years passed, he grew into a strong soldier and a skillful horseman.

As a child, Hannibal swore to be an enemy of Rome for the rest of his life.

MIND AND BODY

Historians tell us that Hannibal was a scholar as well as a soldier. Most Carthaginians considered Greece an enemy. The Barca family valued what the Greeks added to the world's knowledge of science and philosophy. Hannibal was taught to speak Greek by a tutor, who went with him to Spain. It is even said that Hannibal wrote books and speeches in that language. However, nothing he wrote has survived.[11]

The best evidence of what Hannibal looked like is found on silver coins minted in Spain. They show a beardless face. If this image is true, Hannibal also had a straight nose, a strong forehead, and curly hair.[12] He looks much like the image on another coin that is believed to represent his father, Hamilcar.

 ## THE DEATH OF HANNIBAL'S FATHER

For nine years Hamilcar waged war against Spanish tribes. He gained control of territory along the southern coast of Spain, and then continued to push north. An accident ended his command in 228 B.C. Hamilcar drowned while crossing a river.

The Barca family selected Hamilcar's replacement. They chose their son-in-law, Hasdrubal the Handsome (not to be confused with Hannibal's younger brother, also named Hasdrubal). He took command of the Carthaginian army in Spain. The leaders in the Carthage Senate objected. They wanted to pick the new general.

The Barcas influenced military leaders and citizens of Carthage, and the Senate was forced to appoint their relative to command.

Hasdrubal ruled Spain for the next eight years. Under his leadership, Carthage claimed more land there. Its territory stretched as far north as the Ebro River. He built the city of New Carthage, located on the finest harbor along Spain's Mediterranean coast. It became an important settlement. Within the city there were fortifications, palaces, a mint where coins were made, docks, and a weapons store.

Hasdrubal used peaceful means to add territory. He worked to build friendly relations with local tribes. He tried to win the support of native leaders. He also signed a peace treaty with the Romans. In the treaty, Carthage and Rome agreed on a plan. The plan divided Spain between the two powers. The Ebro River in Spain was the boundary between their territories.

In 221 B.C., Hasdrubal was murdered by a local man. Hasdrubal had killed the man's master and he wanted revenge.[13] In Carthage, the Senate prepared to appoint a new commander-in-chief. While they debated, the army in Spain made their own choice. They elected Hannibal. He was now twenty-five years old and ready for this task. He had served under his father and his brother-in-law. Hannibal had done all he could to prepare himself to be a military leader. He had endured heat and cold, fatigue, and hunger with his men. He slept on the ground surrounded by those he led, covered only by a cloak.[14]

Hannibal also showed a knack for battle tactics. If the situation called for enthusiasm and courage, the young soldier led the way. His men respected his fearless fighting style. These qualities earned him the complete loyalty of his soldiers. Hannibal inspired their confidence and they would do anything for him.[15]

The young general needed all the support he could muster. Now in command, he prepared to fulfill his pledge to his father. From the first day he took charge, Livy wrote, Hannibal "acted as if he had definite instructions to take Italy as his sphere of operations and to make war on Rome" and bring the great enemy of Carthage, to its knees.[16]

3

HANNIBAL IN COMMAND

The Carthaginian army was a strange mixture of troops. Only a few officers were citizens of the African city-state. Most of the warriors were mercenaries. They were paid to fight for Carthage. These troops came from many parts of Africa and some were from islands in the Mediterranean. Others came from Spain, France, and even Italy.[1] Under Hannibal, these groups formed a skillful fighting force.

The Carthaginian infantry, or foot soldiers, were heavily armed. They wore iron breastplates and helmets. They carried large shields, cutting swords, and long spears. As they prepared to meet an enemy, the infantry stood shoulder to shoulder. Each man's right side was covered by his neighbor's shield. They pointed their long spears at the enemy, forming a deadly wall.

Hannibal's troops also included slingers armed with slingshots. The sling was usually two cords attached to a pouch. The pouch could hold a large stone. Slings had different length cords so stones could sail over different distances. The cords helped slingers throw rocks farther than they could with their hands. They could throw with great accuracy and reload rapidly.

Two units formed the Carthaginian cavalry. There was the heavy brigade and the light brigade. The heavy brigade was composed of riders mounted on powerful Spanish-bred horses. The soldiers wore armor and carried shields. They also carried a short lance that was two-edged and slightly curved. It could be used to cut like a sword or thrust like a spear.

Horsemen from North Africa rode in Hannibal's light brigade. They used small but tough horses that adapted well to mountain or desert terrain. These soldiers rode without bridles. They controlled their mounts with a rope around the neck and the pressure of their knees. They wore little protective gear. In battle, they wheeled in, or veered close to the enemy, threw their spears, then retreated quickly.

More Spanish Territory

Now that he was in command, Hannibal changed the plan of attack in Spain. He gave up his brother-in-law's peaceful ways of adding new territory. He decided to copy his father's methods. He would use force to expand into new regions. The general marched northward with his mighty army.

Hannibal planned to take control of fertile areas in Spain south of the Ebro River. The treaty with Rome allowed Carthage to control this part of Spain. He stormed towns, and his attacks terrified the citizens. They laid down their arms and surrendered to the

ELEPHANTS IN BATTLE

Hannibal's elephants were African forest elephants. At the shoulder, they measured about eight feet tall. These elephants were identified by their sloping backs, large ears, and ribbed trunks.[2]

African forest elephants were not much bigger than a horse. Coins minted about this time, show the relative size of a rider on an African forest elephant.[3] The smaller size of these animals made it much easier for them to travel across the Alps. Larger Indian elephants would have found it more difficult to lumber along the narrow mountain paths.

Hannibal's elephants frightened the Roman cavalry horses. They disliked the sight, smell, and trumpeting sounds the strange beasts made. Tribesmen also turned and ran when elephants charged. Most had never seen such creatures before.

Carthaginians. Hannibal forced villagers to hand over stores of food and other supplies. He needed an enormous reserve of grain to feed his army when they marched to Rome.

Scouts were also sent ahead to Gaul and Italy. They gathered information about routes across the Alps. They made contact with tribes living along the way. Hannibal wanted to establish friendly relations with them. He would need allies to provide supplies for his army. He also planned to recruit local tribesmen in his fight against Rome.

MORE PREPARATIONS

The following summer, Hannibal pushed north. He gained control over more tribes in territories south of the Ebro. On the march back to New Carthage, he discovered that he had not crushed all the natives in the area. His army was met by a large force of villagers. They had joined together to fight. Hannibal realized that the tribesmen outnumbered his army and might overpower his warriors. He retreated across a wide river and prepared a trap using his war elephants.[4]

The tribesmen followed the Carthaginian Army. They forded the stream. As they climbed out of the water, Hannibal ordered the elephant drivers to charge. The great beasts trampled many tribesmen as they struggled to climb up the riverbank. Their first attack was crushed. Then Hannibal and his army charged. The tribesmen resisted only a short time before they turned and ran. After this show of force, no other tribes resisted.

HUSBAND AND FATHER

After he took command in Spain, Hannibal married a woman named Imilce. She was the daughter of a local chieftain. Her family may have come from Greece. Hannibal and his wife lived together briefly. It is said they had a son and that he was born during the siege of Saguntum. No record exists to confirm his birth. Hannibal probably did not see his wife again after he left on his expedition to Italy.[5]

Now, all of Spain south of the Ebro River, except for the city of Saguntum, was in Carthaginian hands.

SAGUNTUM

Hannibal then set his sights on Saguntum. The city was located about ninety miles south of the Ebro River. It was in territory subject to Carthaginian rule. This had been part of a peace treaty Hasdrubal made with Rome. However, the people of Saguntum were independent and wanted to stay that way. Ten years earlier, they had asked Rome for protection. They knew they would need support if Carthage attacked.[6] Hannibal met with the city's elders. He pressured them to join territories under his rule. Saguntum refused.

In 218 B.C., Saguntum accused a neighboring tribe of raiding its territory. They asked Rome to settle the dispute. They also wanted Rome to protect them from Hannibal. Rome sent a delegation to Saguntum. This official party settled the matter, but it was not a peaceful process. One local group wanted the city to accept Carthaginian rule. Several of these citizens were killed.

The delegation from Rome went to New Carthage. They asked to meet with Hannibal. The Romans demanded that Hannibal follow the treaty of 226 B.C. He was not to march north of the Ebro River. They also warned Hannibal not to attack the city of Saguntum and reminded him it was under Rome's protection.

Hannibal declared that Carthaginian supporters had been killed in Saguntum. It was his duty to even the score for their deaths.[7] The Roman delegation was not satisfied. They sailed to Carthage and protested Hannibal's reaction to the members of the Carthaginian Senate. The delegation insisted that Hannibal be removed from power and handed over to Rome. Carthage refused. The Roman historian Livy recorded the debate between the two groups:

> One Roman delegate laid his hand on the fold of his toga where he had gathered it at his breast . . . "Here." He said "we bring you peace and war. Take which you will."
>
> Scarcely had he spoken when the answer no less proudly rang out: "Whichever you please—we do not care."
>
> The delegate let the gathered folds fall and cried: "We give you war."
>
> The Carthaginian senators replied as one man: "We accept it: and in the same spirit we will fight to the end."[8]

 ## SIEGE OF SAGUNTUM

While Rome and Carthage debated the issue, Hannibal acted. He marched on Saguntum, a walled city set on a hilltop about a mile from the sea. It was a strong position, easily defended from attack. Hannibal invaded the territory, destroying crops in the fields. Then he pitched camp in front of the town and began the siege. The Second Punic War, sometimes called Hannibal's War, had begun.

The general needed to take Saguntum for several reasons. The land around the city was some of the most fertile in Spain. Its capture gave him another source of supplies for his army. Hannibal also wanted to send a reminder of his power to the tribes he controlled. He thought a show of force would keep them in line. Most importantly, he would be able to march toward Italy, leaving no enemy stronghold behind him.[9] Rome protested loudly, but did not send troops to defend Saguntum.

Hannibal stormed the city's walls. He used catapults and battering rams but with little success. The walls were too strong and too high. The troops inside fought back fiercely. They fired missiles at Hannibal's warriors from the towers. Small bands of soldiers even attacked the Carthaginian camp. Though they were outnumbered, the people of Saguntum refused to give up. They gained confidence with each day they kept the enemy outside their walls.

During one clash, Hannibal rode too near the city's wall. He was hit in the thigh by a javelin. The wound was serious. The fighting stopped temporarily until he recovered.

When the fighting began again, Hannibal used all his weapons. He dragged up a wooden tower. Catapults and stone throwers were mounted on the rolling platform. These weapons killed many defenders. Hannibal then ordered troops to attack the wall with picks. Large sections caved in. His warriors scrambled over the rubble and into the city. Hannibal ordered his warriors to kill all men of military age. Finally, those who were still alive surrendered and Hannibal's men ransacked the city.

Many warriors died during the eight-month siege. The spoils and slaves were divided among Hannibal's troops. This was the payment for his soldiers. He also sent valuable plunder back to Carthage to encourage the continued support of the Senate.

When the news of Saguntum's fall reached Rome, members of the Senate were shocked.[10] They had assumed that Hannibal would not attack the city. After all, they had ordered him to leave it alone. Once again, as the Romans debated the situation, Hannibal planned his next move.

 # FINAL PREPARATIONS

Hannibal returned to New Carthage and called a meeting of his Spanish troops. According to Livy, the great general told them:

> Since . . . we are soon to fight a campaign in distant parts and nobody knows when you may see your homes and loved ones again, I have decided to grant a leave of absence to any man who wishes to visit his family. Your orders are to return to duty at the beginning of spring, in order that with God's help, we may begin a war which will fill your pockets with gold and carry your fame to the world's end.[11]

Hannibal then began his preparations. He planned to take the war to Rome. His brother Hasdrubal had joined him in Spain so they could work together. An invasion by sea was impossible in 218 B.C. The treaty signed at the end of the First Punic War made it illegal for Carthage to build a larger fleet. The fleet in New

Carthage was too small to carry the large army to Italy. Hannibal's only option was an overland invasion. This meant marching hundreds of miles through territories held by hostile tribes. It also meant crossing many great rivers and the Italian Alps. Once he reached Italy, Hannibal and his army would be isolated. They would have no home base and no supply sources nearby. Most of the time, they would be forced to fight and live off the land.[12]

Hannibal also realized that while he marched to Italy, Romans might attack Carthage or Spain. He sent additional troops to defend Carthage. Polybius, a Greek historian, wrote that "the troops who crossed to Africa . . . numbered 1,200 horse and 13,850 foot . . ." In

HANNIBAL'S DREAM

One story recounted in Livy's history may or may not be factual, but it is certainly quite a tale. Hannibal had a dream before he marched off to Italy. In the dream, a young man told Hannibal he had been sent by God to guide him. He told the young general to follow him, keeping his eyes always to the front. At first, Hannibal did as he was instructed. He did not look to the right or the left. He did not look back. Then, he grew curious and turned to look around. He saw a monstrous snake gliding along behind him. It knocked over trees and bushes in its path. A storm cloud formed in the sky. Thunder crashed. Hannibal asked his guide what all this meant. A voice answered that it showed the destruction of Italy.[13]

addition, "there were 870 slingers."[14] Polybius wrote a history of the Punic Wars called *The Rise of the Roman Empire*.

Hannibal placed his brother Hasdrubal Barca in command in Spain. He left 15,000 men, 21 elephants, and 50 warships to defend that territory, according to Polybius. He claimed he found these figures on a bronze tablet in the southern part of Italy. Hannibal himself is said to have made the list.[15]

With Carthage and Spain reinforced, Hannibal was ready. The time had finally come to invade Italy.

4

THE MARCH TO ITALY BEGINS

Hannibal set out from New Carthage near the end of May 218 B.C. He divided his army of ninety thousand foot soldiers and twelve thousand cavalry into three divisions.[1] They marched north toward the Ebro River. They traveled as quickly as such a large force could. Though he had not told his men where they were headed, Hannibal wanted to cross the Alps before Rome learned he was on the move. If his plan worked, the Second Punic War would be fought on the Italian peninsula.

By July, Hannibal and his army crossed the Ebro River. He sent a scouting party ahead to Gaul. They were to explore passages across the Alps and to win the good will of tribes along the route, using bribes if necessary.

Hannibal was now in territory claimed by Rome. He pressured tribes that lived in the hilly countryside to

A Boatload of Elephants

Elephants are not mentioned as a part of the force Hannibal set off with in May. He needed to move swiftly if his army was to reach the Alps before winter. Elephants would have slowed his progress. It is likely that these great beasts were loaded on ships and carried by sea to Emporion in southern Gaul.[2] The city was about seventy-five miles northeast of modern-day Barcelona, Spain. This port was as close to Italy as Hannibal dared to take the elephants by sea. He did not want the Roman fleet to capture them. At that point, the elephants joined the Carthaginian army and marched over the Alps with Hannibal.

submit to Carthage. They refused to give in without a fight. The general had to control this region. Once he reached Italy, messengers would need to travel back and forth along this route. Without control of this area, Hannibal could not be sure his orders would reach his brother in New Carthage.

He also could not let the tribes' resistance slow his army down. Hannibal attacked the fortified towns. He drove his soldiers hard. Many were lost during the fierce battles. After a month of fighting, most tribes were crushed by the might of the Carthaginian army.

Hannibal knew he had to station troops in the region. The tribesmen would remain loyal only as long as the Carthaginians seemed to be strong. He left his brother Hanno in charge of one thousand cavalry and ten thousand foot soldiers.[3] They were to guard the passes between Spain and Gaul. These passes would be the communication line between Hannibal and New Carthage.

By this time, Hannibal's troops realized where they were headed. Many were alarmed by the length of the march and the thought of crossing the Alps. Three thousand soldiers refused to go on. Hannibal dismissed four thousand more warriors who seemed uneasy about his plan.[4] He also decided to leave many of his provisions behind with Hanno. If he reduced the amount of food and supplies carried by his pack train, they could move faster. It was late summer and crops were ready to be harvested in areas the army would march through. They could live off the land.

The Carthaginian army left Spain behind. They climbed into the Pyrenees mountains. The route Hannibal took is uncertain. Historians have debated the possibilities. He might have crossed over the 1,100-foot Col DeBanyuls pass. But there are others he could have used. By the time they reached the Pyrenees, Hannibal's army had covered nearly half the distance in terms of miles, but the most difficult part of the march was still ahead.[5]

Hannibal camped on the other side of the pass in southern Gaul. He rested his troops and reorganized. His elephants most likely arrived about this time and joined the army.

FEEDING AN ARMY ON THE MOVE

Hannibal left New Carthage with an enormous number of warriors and pack animals loaded with heavy baggage. Keeping everyone moving was difficult during the long march. The army probably traveled less than ten miles a day.

It was also a challenge to feed so many people and animals. No historian recorded information about how Hannibal fed three divisions and all the pack animals during his march. South of the Ebro River, he probably had storehouses with supplies in friendly villages. North of the river, the villagers were hostile. It is more likely that all supplies had to be carried on pack animals.

By the time Hannibal crossed the Pyrenees into Gaul, the size of this army had shrunk. Even then, it numbered about nine thousand cavalry and fifty thousand foot soldiers. This was still a huge number to feed and keep moving.[6]

ACROSS SOUTHERN GAUL

Hannibal's scouts told tribes in Gaul that the army only wanted to march through to Italy. However, news that Carthaginians had occupied country in Spain beyond the Pyrenees worried the local people.[7] They did not want to be slaves of the African city-state. Several tribes took up arms and prepared for battle.

Hannibal did not want more fighting to delay his march. He asked the village chieftains for a conference and they agreed. Hannibal assured the tribes that he had come to Gaul as a friend, not as an enemy. He told them that he had no wish to draw a sword before he was in Italy. This statement, along with gifts, satisfied the chieftains. The Carthaginian army marched on quickly. They covered nearly one hundred eighty miles before coming to another obstacle that slowed them down—the Rhone River.

CROSSING THE RHONE

Hannibal camped on the west bank of the river to plan his crossing. At that point the Rhone was nearly two-thirds of a mile wide (one kilometer) and about nine feet deep. It would be no easy task to transport thousands of troops, cavalry horses, and forty elephants from one side to the other.

Many tribesmen in the area were willing to help Hannibal. He encouraged their friendship with gifts. These villagers were traders. They traveled up and down the river in boats, selling their goods. Hannibal paid to use their boats and to have more boats built. Anything that floated and could carry a load was put to use. The natives built rafts and hollowed out tree trunks. They worked quickly. They were eager to see Hannibal across the river as soon as possible.[8] His huge army was devouring food supplies they had stored for the winter. Within two days, Hannibal had enough rafts for all his soldiers and their gear. They were ready to cross the Rhone River.

🐘 TROUBLE AHEAD

Unfortunately, the Carthaginian warriors would need to be ready for battle when they reached the opposite side. Not all tribal members had agreed to help Hannibal. Some had crossed to the eastern bank of the river. They were prepared to fight to keep the Carthaginian army from advancing.

Under cover of night, Hannibal sent a small band of troops twenty-five miles upstream. Here an island split the river into two channels. The water was shallower at this spot, making it easier to cross. Some soldiers hollowed out logs to use as rafts. Others swam across with their shields beneath them and their clothes stuffed in leather bags. The rest crossed on rafts lashed together to form a bridge.[9] After the crossing was completed, they made camp and rested overnight.

The next morning, the small band marched downstream. As they drew near the place Hannibal waited with the rest of the army, they sent up a smoke signal. The signal let the general know they were not far away and ready for action. When Hannibal spotted the smoke, he ordered his troops to cross the Rhone.

The infantrymen used the boats, rafts, and hollowed out trees. Most of the cavalry swam across beside their horses. Some horses were tied to boats to make the crossing. Others were ferried across, saddled and bridled, ready for riders to mount instantly on the opposite shore.

As Hannibal's army started crossing, the tribesmen surged down to the edge of the water. They howled at the flotilla of rafts coming toward them. They shook their shields above their heads and waved their spears. They were ready to attack the first soldiers to step onshore. Then, the tribesmen heard a noise behind them—shouts of the small band of Carthaginians that had crossed the river the day before. The natives soon realized they were trapped. Thousands of armed men would soon land on the riverbank, while a band of soldiers attacked them from the rear. They fought back briefly, then broke and ran. Most returned to their villages to hide. Hannibal's foot soldiers and cavalry completed crossing the Rhone without any more trouble. After this skirmish, Hannibal realized he had little to fear from tribes in Gaul.[10]

ELEPHANTS CROSS THE RHONE

Next, Hannibal made plans to move his elephants across the river. Several methods may have been used. According to one account, recorded by Livy, "the beasts were herded close to the bank, and a . . . ferocious one was goaded [annoyed] by his driver."[11] The driver then jumped into the river and swam for his life. The angry elephant chased the driver and the rest of the herd followed. The current carried them to the opposite bank of the river.[12]

It is more likely that they were ferried across on rafts. Hannibal's men built floating piers about two hundred feet long and fifty feet wide. The piers stretched out into the river where the current was strong. To keep these floating structures from being pushed downstream,

Hannibal had ropes tied to the piers and attached to trees on shore.

Rafts of the same width and half as long were fastened to the end of the piers. To support the weight of the elephants, floats were lashed on the sides of the rafts. The piers and rafts were then covered with earth. Drivers hoped this would make the elephants believe they were still on dry land. With females in the lead, a few of the great beasts were driven onto a pier. As soon as they stepped on the raft, ropes that held it in place were cast off. The load of elephants was then towed across the river by men rowing boats.

Some of the elephants panicked, stampeded, and tipped their rafts. They fell into the water. Fortunately, by then they had floated beyond the deepest part of the river. The water was shallow enough for the elephants to hold their trunks up over the surface of the water. They waded across safely. Not a single elephant was lost.

With all of his army on the left bank of the Rhone, Hannibal made camp. The next morning scouts brought him some bad news. A Roman fleet was anchored at the mouth of the Rhone River. Troops had come ashore and were moving upstream toward the Carthaginian camp. Hannibal immediately sent five hundred cavalry to watch the Romans and report on their activity.

5

Rome Prepares for War

When the Romans learned of the fall of Saguntum, there was no debate about whether or not to invade Spain and Carthage. This attack on an ally was treated as an act of war.[1] They had warned Hannibal a year before to leave the city alone. However, by this time, the Carthaginian army was already on the march. It had crossed the Ebro River and was on the way to Italy before the Roman fleet sailed.

Each year two new consuls were elected in Rome. They commanded the Roman legions, or armies. In 218 B.C., Tiberious Sempronius Longus and Publius Cornelius Scipio were chosen as consuls. Longus was sent to Sicily. He was to plan an attack on Carthage. Scipio was ordered to Spain. His orders were to stop Hannibal.

Scipio and his legions sailed to Spain on sixty ships. Along the way, he learned that the Carthaginian army had crossed the Pyrenees. His primary goal was to stop

ROME'S CITIZEN ARMY

Rome's army was led by two consuls. They served as commanders for one-year terms. The consuls selected men to fill four new legions. Each legion numbered 4,200 soldiers. The consuls called all males between seventeen and forty-six to an assembly which usually took place in the month of March. Soldiers were picked from this group of citizens. This made the Roman army quite different from Hannibal's mercenary army.

All citizens of Rome had to serve six years in the legions. During war, this service was likely to be done all at one time. When all was peaceful, soldiers might take a year or two off, then return to service. Soldiers were also expected to supply their own equipment. Warriors were assigned to serve in the cavalry or infantry. In addition, Rome's allies had to supply men to serve with the citizen legions.

In 218 B.C., Scipio raised two legions before he sailed for Spain. He had two thousand two hundred cavalry and twenty-two thousand foot soldiers.

Hannibal, so he abandoned his plans to sail to Spain. The Roman fleet anchored near the mouth of the Rhone River and the army went ashore. The warriors spent several days recovering from the sea voyage and preparing for battle.

Scipio believed Hannibal was many miles away. He expected the hostile tribes and difficult terrain in southern Gaul to slow him down. When he learned that his enemy was just miles upstream on the banks of the Rhone River, he was amazed.[2]

The Roman consul sent out three hundred of his best horsemen. They were to gather more information. Hannibal also sent scouts to spy on the Romans. The two parties bumped into each other. A fight broke out. Many were killed or wounded. The Romans lost about one hundred sixty warriors. The Africans lost more than two hundred. Finally, Hannibal's scouts turned and fled. The Roman force chased the horsemen back to their camp. They took a count of Hannibal's forces before reporting back to Scipio.

Scipio listened to information gathered by his scouting party. Then he prepared to march up the Rhone River to attack. When he reached the place where Hannibal had crossed, he found the camp deserted. The Carthaginians had marched north three days earlier. They left one day after the cavalry skirmish.

Scipio found it hard to believe that the Carthaginian general planned to cross the Alps. He knew it meant marching across wild regions controlled by unfriendly tribes. But he now guessed that was what Hannibal intended to do.[3] Scipio also realized his army could not catch up to the Carthaginians. He had left all his stores and equipment with the ships. There was no time to arrange for food to supply his army or the pack animals needed to transport it overland. The Roman army turned around and marched back to the mouth of the Rhone River.

Scipio loaded his troops back on ships. He ordered them on to Spain with his brother in command. They

THE ROMAN SOLDIERS

The Romans had a strong infantry. These foot soldiers were divided into four classes. The youngest, poorest citizens served as *velites*. This Latin word meant "lightly armored." Their job was to attack the enemy first. They carried four-foot-long javelins, swords, and wicker shields covered with animal hide. The javelins allowed them to strike from a distance, and their swords were used for close combat.

The next class of infantry was the *hastate*. This meant "with a hasta," the kind of spear they carried. These soldiers were in top condition, but young and inexperienced. Most wore a square breastplate that offered some protection. They served as the second line of defense.

The older, more experienced soldiers were called the *principes*, meaning leaders. They were armed with javelins and swords. They carried oval shields.

The *triarii* made up the last infantry class. These were veteran soldiers. They were not used in battle unless all else had failed. Triarii carried long thrusting spears. These veterans formed a protective line at the rear. They would kneel on one leg, rest shields on their shoulders, and point spears upward.

The triarii, principes, and the hastate all wore bronze helmets with crests of red or black feathers on top. These feathers made the soldiers look taller and more intimidating. They also helped commanders spot their warriors during fierce battles.

Roman legions had small cavalry units. The skills of the Roman riders and the quality of the horses were poor. At the beginning of the war, Roman units were no match for Hannibal's experienced and highly skilled cavalry.

were to cut off Hannibal's supply line. Then Scipio sailed back to Italy. The consul felt his first job was to stop Hannibal. He intended to join troops stationed near the Italian Alps and then wait. He would be ready for what was left of Hannibal's army when it reached Italy, if a force of any size survived.

Hannibal's Allies From Italy

Visitors arrived at Hannibal's camp on the Rhone River. They were chieftains from villages directly over the Alps in Italy. Their lived on the plains of the Po River. The chieftains promised to fight with Hannibal against the Romans. They also offered to guide the Carthaginian army over the mountains. They claimed to know a route that would take him across the Alps quickly and safely.

Before marching on, Hannibal needed to boost the morale of his warriors. They were worried about what lay ahead. They remembered how the Romans had defeated Carthage in the First Punic War. They dreaded the march over the Alps. Hannibal's army had been told many stories about these mountains. Many of the tales were horrible. They frightened even the bravest of warriors.[4]

Hannibal called all his troops together and spoke to them. Livy recorded the following speech in his history, although it is unlikely that these are Hannibal's exact words. The account does show how the general may have inspired his men to go on.

> What sudden panic is this which has entered those
> breasts where fear has never been? Year after year you

have fought with me, and won . . . you were justly angry and crossed the Ebro bent upon obliterating the very name of Rome and setting the world free. Then . . . none of you thought . . . the journey long. . . . but now, when you can see that much the greater part of the distance is already behind you . . . when, finally you have the Alps in sight, and know that the other side of them is Italian soil; now I repeat, at the very gateway of the enemy's country, you come to a halt—exhausted! What do you think the Alps *are*? Are they anything worse than high mountains? Say, if you will, that they are higher than the Pyrenees, but what of it? No part of earth reaches the sky . . . If a small party can cross them, surely armies can? . . . with nothing to carry but their military gear . . .[5]

Hannibal ended by reminding his men of their goal: "It is . . . now . . . Rome, the mightiest city of the world, you aim to conquer . . . [so] steel your hearts to march forward, to halt only . . . [at] the walls of Rome."[6]

The army applauded loudly when he finished speaking. They were encouraged, ready to go on.[7] Hannibal ordered his men to rest and prepare to march the next day.

ON TO THE ALPS

As Hannibal finished addressing his warriors, some of his scouting party returned. Many had not survived the skirmish with the Romans. Those who could still ride galloped into camp. They were fleeing for their lives. The Romans followed close behind. The scouts quickly told Hannibal what had happened.

Hannibal considered taking action against Scipio and the Roman legions. But he decided to march on toward the Alps instead. The next morning, the Carthaginian army moved north, following the Rhone River. This was not the most direct route to the mountains, but Hannibal wanted to put some distance between his warriors and the Romans. This made another unplanned skirmish unlikely. The general also wanted his warriors to concentrate on the next challenge they faced—the Italian Alps.

The army marched for four days. When Hannibal gave his men another rest, a local tribe asked him to

HANNIBAL DECIDES TO FLEE, NOT FIGHT

Livy, the Roman historian, wrote that Hannibal considered fighting Scipio on the Rhone where he had the advantage. After all, his army outnumbered the Roman legions. Polybius, the Greek historian, wrote, however, that the Carthaginian general immediately led his army north along the river. Hannibal most likely marched off to avoid a battle in Gaul. Another battle would have delayed his journey. Hannibal believed it was more important to fight and win in Italy, on Roman territory.[8]

Hannibal had also left most of his supply train behind in Spain. He had to forage from the nearby villages to feed his men and horses. Such a large force soon consumed everything that could be found in one location. He could not keep his army in any one place for more than a few days or food supplies simply ran out.[9]

The Alps are a hard terrain for people to cross even today. Hannibal did not have any modern technology to help him. He had to get not only his soldiers but also dozens of horses and elephants across the dangerous mountain range.

settle a quarrel. Two brothers both wanted to be the village chief. Hannibal sided with Braneus, the elder brother. Braneus was grateful and gave the Carthaginian army food and grain. He also gave them boots and warm clothing needed to survive in the mountains. When Hannibal marched off, the new chief ordered his tribesmen to protect the Carthaginians from any attack on their way to the Alps.[10]

At last, Hannibal reached the Alps. The days were growing shorter and temperatures were getting colder. These signs told him winter was not far away. Hannibal had wanted to reach the mountains earlier, but the siege of Saguntum had delayed his departure from Spain. Now the Carthaginian army began the ascent of the Alps, and it soon faced new dangers.

6

HANNIBAL ROUTS THE ROMANS

The run-in with Scipio's warriors in southern Gaul spoiled Hannibal's plan to surprise the Romans. The consul guessed where Hannibal was heading. When the Carthaginian army marched into northern Italy in 218 B.C., Roman legions were already waiting. They were prepared to stop their enemy.

Hannibal camped at the base of the Alps in the Po River Valley. His army was exhausted. The trek over rough mountain tracks had been grueling. It had been impossible to carry enough provisions for thousands of warriors. They had often gone hungry. He gave his men and horses time to rest. They needed to regain their strength before moving on.[1]

Meanwhile, Hannibal made contact with people that lived in the area. He offered them peace and friendship. The Romans had recently conquered many of these groups of people. Some welcomed the Carthaginians, but others did not. Hannibal attacked those that refused his offer. He surrounded the largest village in the area. After three days, the tribe surrendered. The general killed everyone who resisted him—a brutal act, but not unusual for that time.[2] Other nearby tribes soon pledged their support to the Carthaginian army.

By now, Scipio had reached the Po River. He was surprised to discover Hannibal in control of areas in Italy. He expected most of the African army to die while crossing the Alps.[3] The Senate immediately sent word to their second consul, Longus, who was waiting in Sicily. His troops were ready to go where needed. They ordered Longus to sail for northern Italy.

Meanwhile, Scipio bridged the Ticino River, a tributary of the Po River. Hannibal's army was camped a few miles away. The Romans crossed and sent troops to check their enemy's position. Hannibal and his own cavalry were also out on a scouting mission. Both parties spotted clouds of dust created by riders. They stopped and prepared for battle.

Hannibal advanced with six thousand horsemen. Scipio called out his spearmen and two thousand riders. Hannibal's cavalry struck and the spearmen broke and fled. For a time, the two cavalry forces seemed evenly matched. Then the Carthaginians circled the Roman troops. They attacked from the rear. Scipio was wounded during the battle. His seventeen-year-old son and a Ligurian slave helped rescue him. The Roman cavalry formed a screen around the consul and he was carried back to camp. Clearly, Hannibal's cavalry would be difficult to defeat.[4]

Hannibal and Scipio Africanus in battle

 # THE ROMANS RETREAT

Scipio broke camp and marched back to the Ticino River. He wanted to get his legions across the floating bridge before the Carthaginians caught up with them.

The consul escaped with most of his force. Hannibal and his army followed the Romans. They captured about six hundred Roman warriors that had stayed behind to break up the bridge. The Romans had already destroyed both ends so Hannibal's army could not cross, but that did not stop the Carthaginian general. He was determined to follow the retreating Roman army.

 # HANNIBAL IN PURSUIT

Hannibal marched in the opposite direction up the Po. He needed a place to cross the river. After two days he

ELEPHANTS AT WORK?

Some say that Hannibal ordered his cavalry and infantry to swim across the Ticino River near the bridge destroyed by Scipio's retreating forces. He used a line of elephants to slow the river's current. Then the general led the rest of his troops up stream.

"But anyone who knows the Po will find this account hard to believe," wrote Roman historian Livy. Foot soldiers might have swum across using something as a float. Livy goes on to state that it was unlikely that mounted troops could have made headway in the "strong current without losing their horses and gear."[5]

found a spot and built his own bridge. While his army crossed, the general met with messengers from nearby villages. They came to declare support for the Carthaginians. They agreed to furnish supplies and send men to serve. Hannibal received them warmly.[6] Then, he led his army back downstream after his enemy.

Meanwhile, Scipio had camped in what he believed was a safe place. He made sure his wounded soldiers were cared for and tended his own injuries. But two days later, the Carthaginians arrived. Hannibal lined up his army for battle in full view of the Romans. They refused to attack him, so he pitched camp about six miles away.

ROMAN DESERTERS

That night, trouble broke out in Scipio's camp. Many tribesmen serving in the legion were Gauls who lived nearby. They seized their arms and attacked the sleeping Romans. They killed and wounded many men. They cut off the heads of those they had murdered. Then they deserted to the Carthaginian camp. Other Gauls from the area had already joined Hannibal.

Scipio retreated again the next night. This time he moved back to hills that could easily be defended. He fortified his position. He had his men dig a trench and build a palisade, or wall. Then Scipio waited for Consul Longus and his troops to arrive. Hannibal followed, so as not to lose contact with the Romans. He again camped a few miles away. By this time, he was in need of food. He demanded the grain Romans had stored in a neighboring settlement. Hannibal was preparing to attack when the villagers handed over the food supply for four hundred gold pieces.[7]

REINFORCEMENTS ARRIVE

Consul Longus arrived with reinforcements for Scipio's forces. All Rome's armies were in northern Italy. They planned to stop Hannibal's army from advancing. Longus wanted to attack immediately, but Scipio urged him to proceed with caution.[8]

Hannibal continued to raid the countryside. Tribes who lived nearby were unwilling to side with Rome or Carthage. They wanted to see who would win the battle. This angered Hannibal, who expected these tribes to support him. Many of them had sent envoys inviting Hannibal to Italy to free them from Rome. His resentment, and the need for provisions, prompted him to send troops to forage for food and supplies.[9]

The raids forced the tribes to choose a side. They sent a delegation to the two Roman consuls. The tribes begged for protection. Scipio was unwilling to send troops because he did not trust the tribes. Longus felt military aid would keep the tribes loyal to Rome.[10] He sent out his cavalry and a thousand spearmen. His force surprised Hannibal's raiders, who were scattered over the countryside, loaded down with plunder. Many were killed but some managed to reach the Carthaginian camp safely. Hannibal sent reinforcements to stop the Romans' advance. Longus believed he had won the battle. Over Scipio's protest, he prepared for action without delay.

 ## PLAN OF ATTACK

Meanwhile, Hannibal planned a trap for the Roman legions. He found a place where a small band of troops could hide. It was on a steep stream bank with heavy vegetation that provided cover for troops. Livy recorded the instruction Hannibal gave his brother Mago: "This is the spot you must occupy. Choose a hundred men from the infantry and a hundred from the cavalry."[11] Mago's force hid during the night. Early the next morning, Hannibal sent his light cavalry to attack. Once the fight was on, they were to pull back, making sure the Romans followed.

Longus immediately advanced with all his riders and six thousand infantry when Hannibal's cavalry attacked his guards. The rest of the army followed. It was a snowy winter day. The men and horses set out early, without eating or getting warm. They felt the effects of the cold immediately. Soon they had to ford a river and the cold water numbed them. They could hardly hold their weapons after struggling across.[12]

Meanwhile, most of Hannibal's army was warming itself by great fires. They ate a hearty breakfast. When word came that the Romans were across the river, the Carthaginians fell into formation.

Hannibal massed his infantry in the middle of his line. He placed his cavalry on either side. The elephants lined up beyond them. The infantry's attack almost overwhelmed the cold, exhausted Romans. Hannibal's elephants charged through the enemy line. Roman cavalry horses bolted in terror. Then, Hannibal sprang his trap, a tactic he used often. Mago and two hundred troops closed in from the rear. For a while the Romans held their line, even against the elephants. Foot soldiers armed with javelins drove the huge beasts off, stabbing them in the soft skin under their tails.[13] The pain panicked the elephants. When they turned on Hannibal's troops, he removed them from the battle.

By then, the Carthaginians had the Romans surrounded. They escaped by hacking their way through Hannibal's line, retreating to the river. Many were killed as they stood on the bank. More drowned trying to swim across. Others scattered over the countryside. Hannibal did not pursue his enemy across the river. The Carthaginians returned to camp. They were so cold they

Hannibal's elephants often crushed attacking Roman soldiers. The Romans would sometimes overcome the elephants, but the animals still inspired fear in many of the Roman troops.

could hardly enjoy the victory. The Battle of Trebia was over and Hannibal had won.

The following night, the Roman consuls marched quietly away. Scipio prepared to winter in a safe location in northern Italy. Longus rode south to Rome to report what had happened. The news of this defeat caused panic in the capital city. People feared Hannibal would arrive at the city gates at any moment.[14]

THE FIRST WINTER IN ITALY

A Roman poet, Florus, compared Hannibal and his force to a "thunderbolt which had burst its way through the middle of the Alps and descended upon Italy as if

REPLACING ARMS AND RECRUITING WARRIORS

Hannibal was operating in a foreign land. He needed to replace weapons and equipment. He depended on what could be picked up from the battlefield or coaxed from enemies of Rome.

He also needed to replace warriors lost in battle. Hannibal had only a few sources for reinforcements. He could draw troops from tribes that considered Rome their enemy. These tribes lived in the Po Valley and in central and southern Italy. He also planned for more African and Spanish soldiers to join him. But the Roman navy still controlled the Mediterranean Sea, so troops could not come by ship. They would have to march overland, following his route across the Alps.

Roman legions reclaimed much of northern Spain only a few months after Hannibal had gained control. His brother Hanno had been pushed out of the territory. The Carthaginian supply line was cut. Sending orders to his brother Hasdrubal in New Carthage was difficult. All this happened by the end of Hannibal's first summer in Italy.

launched from the skies."[15] The Roman people put up little resistance after this second battle. He moved about the territory freely. His army raided towns, foraging for supplies.

Hannibal also attacked an important Roman trading post. It was near Placentia, the city where the Roman legions were wintering. The post was fortified and well guarded. During the raid, Hannibal was wounded. He left the battle, and the assault failed.

Only a few days later, before his wound healed, Hannibal attacked another post. This time he easily overcame the thirty-five thousand citizens who tried to protect their homes. They surrendered after one day. The Carthaginians plundered the post. They raped, tortured, and killed citizens. Hannibal punished the people there for resisting. He hoped this example might cause others to surrender without a fight.

Hannibal prepared to winter in northern Italy. The climate was much colder than the Africans were used to. His army suffered from the cold and damp. By spring 217 B.C., his horses were in poor condition. All the elephants died, except one.[16] Even with all these problems, Hannibal prepared to raid new territory.

ANOTHER VICTORIOUS SEASON

In spring 217 B.C., Hannibal ordered his army to march. They slipped around the Roman legions that were blocking the main roads to the east and south. The Carthaginians headed for Tuscany in the central plains of Italy. The warriors were eager to raid Roman villages in the area that were rich in grains and cattle.[1]

Hannibal and his army crossed a ridge of the Apennine Mountains, and then dropped into a river valley. It was extremely marshy. No patch of ground was dry enough to make camp. The army was forced to wade through water for three days and nights. Many pack animals fell in the mud and died. Wherever they fell, men piled on the carcasses.[2] This was the only place they could lie down out of the water to sleep.

Hannibal rode across the marshes on his last surviving elephant. This kept him out of the water, but he could not sleep. The damp air affected him badly and he developed an infection in his eyes. There was no place to rest and recover. Hannibal lost the sight in one of his eyes because of this illness.[3]

THE ROMAN CONSUL

The Roman legions were commanded by two newly-elected consuls. One of the consuls was Gaius Flaminius. He set off after the Carthaginians. He wanted to gain fame as the defender of Rome. Many of his officers advised him not to attack the enemy without support from the second consul. Flaminius refused to listen.[4]

When Hannibal learned the Romans were marching after him, he set another trap near Lake Trasimeno. He stationed his army on hills near the lake. The terrain formed a perfect trap. The lakeshore prevented escape in one direction. The hills enclosed the other three sides. Hannibal placed his best troops along the ridge. This forced the Romans to attack up the slope. It was one of Hannibal's favorite tactics. He stationed some local allies and the heavy cavalry on slopes that ran down to the lake. On the flat ground below the hills, his slingers and pikesmen lined up. Then the Carthaginian army waited, ready to spring the trap.

Flaminius made camp on the far side of Lake Trasimeno. He knew Hannibal was nearby. At dawn, he ordered his troops to advance. He wanted to attack before the Carthaginians could get away. They marched through a thick fog that covered the plain. The mist was thinner on the hillsides. The Carthaginians could see each other clearly from their positions.

Hannibal waited until the consul's troops engaged his front line. Then trumpets signaled the Carthaginian infantry and heavy cavalry to strike. They came thundering down the hillside, closing in around the legions' rear guard. They charged at almost the same instant. The Carthaginian attack took the Romans completely by surprise.

The Roman legions had no time to get ready for battle. The Carthaginians struck again and again. They drove the Romans back toward the lake. Many were killed as they waded into the shallow water. For three hours the battle raged. The Carthaginians lost only twenty-five hundred warriors. Fifteen thousand Romans died, including the consul Flaminius. About six thousand Roman troops escaped but were captured the next day.[5]

Hannibal divided the prisoners into two groups—Romans and their allies. He sent the allies home with a message. Carthage was at war with Rome, not with them. These allies were from independent territories. They had signed treaties with Rome. In return, Rome expected allies to send warriors to fight as part of its army. Hannibal hoped some allies would decide to support Carthage instead. The captured Romans were given to Hannibal's warriors to be kept as slaves. This battle was Rome's greatest defeat since the start of hostilities with the Carthaginian Empire.

A Second Disaster

This defeat at Lake Trasimeno was followed quickly by another. The second Roman consul, Servilius, came to help his partner. He sent four thousand cavalry on ahead. His foot soldiers followed several miles behind. Reports of the battle reached the horsemen. They decided to retreat, but not soon enough. Hannibal's riders surrounded them. All were killed or captured.

The loss of his cavalry left Servilius without scouts. He had no way of knowing where Hannibal and his army were. He could not move for fear of bumping into the enemy unexpectedly.

Hannibal was free to roam and pillage wherever he wanted, but even after these two victories he did not march on Rome. The capital city would have to be taken by siege. Hannibal did not have the weapons he needed for this kind of warfare. He had no storming towers, battering rams, or catapults. All were needed to bring down the walls of cities and garrisons.[6] In addition, Hannibal had another problem. He had expected Rome's allies to desert them. So far not one had promised their support to him. They remained loyal to Rome and Hannibal knew they would come to the city's aid if he attacked.

Rome Reacts

Rome had lost the protection of both her armies. The citizenry reacted by electing Quintus Fabius Maximus as dictator. Fabius expected Hannibal to march on Rome.

Siege Warfare and Siege Machines

A siege is a prolonged blockade and attack on a city or fortress. Warriors surround a target and cut off supplies. In addition, they try to break down the palisade or defensive walls. During Hannibal's time, armies used siege towers, battering rams, and catapults to capture fortified cities.

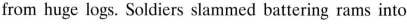

A siege tower is a raised platform that could be moved up to a wall. Attackers climbed the tower. They used it to scale the walls and get inside the city.

Battering rams are often made from huge logs. Soldiers slammed battering rams into

city gates and sections of wall, trying to break them apart.

A catapult is a weapon used to throw missiles over barriers such as walls of stone or dirt. In ancient times, the missiles fired could be spears, rocks, or burning objects. Early catapults were designed like a crossbow but much larger in size.

He prepared the city and its citizens for attack. The city strengthened its walls and towers and destroyed bridges over nearby rivers.

Fabius took over the two legions of the consul Servilius and raised troops for two others. He sent orders to all the people living in areas that Hannibal would march through on his way to Rome. They were to abandon their farms, burn the buildings, and destroy the crops. He wanted them to leave nothing that would aid the enemy.[7]

Fabius also took a new approach to the war with Carthage. He refused to confront Hannibal, avoiding another defeat. The dictator would fight, but only on his terms. Fabius planned to harass his enemy, for example, by attacking small raiding parties. He hoped to slowly reduce the strength of the Carthaginian army. This tactic earned him the nickname "the delayer."

HANNIBAL MOVES

Meanwhile, Hannibal moved his troops to the east coast of Italy. His army was loaded with booty gathered from the battlefield and surrounding territories. They had seized food supplies and herds of cattle. When they reached the coast of the Adriatic Sea, the army rested and rebuilt its strength.

Among the loot Hannibal collected were weapons and armor. He re-equipped his men. He trained them to use the Roman arms. Dictator Fabius followed Hannibal, keeping his men at a safe distance. He sent

---

> ## HANNIBAL SEEKS AID AND NEWS
>
> While on the Italian coast, Hannibal sent messengers by sea. He probably used ships captured on the coast. He needed to report to Carthage. He also wanted to know what was happening in Spain.
>
> When news arrived, Hannibal learned that Rome now controlled the northern part of Spain. His brother Hanno had moved south of the Ebro River for the winter. Hannibal's overland route for messengers, supplies, and reinforcements had been cut off.

out troops to stop Carthaginian raiding parties, but made it clear he would not do battle.

Hannibal's warriors were strong and his horses healthy when he marched again. He set out for the plains south of Rome on Italy's west coast. He had to gain control of a port. With access to the sea, he could send messages to Carthage. Supplies and reinforcements he needed could also be shipped to him from Africa and Spain via the Carthaginian navy.

Hannibal first marched to Capua. It was one of the richest cities in Italy. He made camp there so that the citizens would think he planned to stay indefinitely. The general then sent cavalry units out to forage. He hoped to force Fabius, who had trailed slowly after him, to attack. If he could destroy this Roman army, Hannibal believed Capua and seaports around the gulf of Naples would come over to his side.[8]

A Trap for Hannibal

Fabius did not attack. Instead he blocked the three passes Hannibal could use to leave the area. It was late summer. The land was not suitable for winter quarters. Fabius knew the Carthaginians had to move and thought he had them trapped.[9]

Hannibal decided to advance to the Romans' hilltop fort. He was ready for battle, but Fabius still refused to fight. Hannibal ordered his men to gather wooden torches. They tied the torches to the horns of two thousand cattle. After dark, the herd was driven up a ridge above the pass guarded by the Roman army. A band of infantry followed. When the herd was in place, the Carthaginians lit the torches. The blazing cattle ran wildly through the night. Roman troops guarding the pass saw lights on the ridge above them. Certain they were under attack, they set out to meet the threat. The Romans soon discovered it was a clever trick. The soldiers they thought they saw were only cattle. As the Romans tried to return to their posts, the Carthaginian infantry cut them down. Fabius heard the uproar, but sent no troops until daylight.[10] Meanwhile, Hannibal's army escaped. They went over the pass under the cover of darkness.

The Summer's Last Battle

Hannibal then marched toward Rome. He wanted to force Fabius to attack. When this plan did not work, he moved back across the Apennines. It was time to find winter quarters. He seized a storehouse and built a fortified camp.

Fabius followed Hannibal, camping nearby and pestering his enemy. That fall, he was called back to Rome. Fabius left Marcus Minucius Rufu in command. The new commander continued to send bands of cavalry and light troops out. They attacked the Carthaginian raiding parties, killing many. This encouraged Minucius to attack the enemy camp. Most of Hannibal's army was spread out across the countryside. Only a few warriors were on guard in camp and they were outnumbered by the Romans. Minucius saw his advantage. He attacked and Hannibal almost lost the battle. A large party of Carthaginian troops returned to camp just in time. They drove the Romans back and prevented a disaster.

FABIUS RECALLED TO ROME

The Roman Senate sent for Fabius. He had disappointed every soldier and citizen. They did not like the way he was operating.[11] It had always been Roman practice to seek out the enemy. Then they used the skill and discipline of their warriors to beat them. Now the legions trailed slowly after Hannibal's army.[12] Fabius would not attack. Resentment grew as the Carthaginians raided and burned the countryside.

News reached Rome of the attack of Minucius on Hannibal's camp. Some Senate members wanted to replace Fabius. Instead, they voted to have Fabius and Minucius share the command.[13]

Hannibal now realized Minucius could be drawn into battle. He planned another ambush. The Roman commander took the bait. Minucius sent legions to strike at the Carthaginian troops. Hannibal stationed troops on a hilltop. He kept sending reinforcements to hold the position. His warriors pushed the Roman legions down the hill. Then Hannibal sprang his trap. He had more troops hidden near the base of the hill. These fresh warriors joined the battle. It seemed Hannibal had won again, and then Fabius arrived. He had returned from Rome with more warriors. The Carthaginians were forced to pull back.

Hannibal built a stockade, or fort, around the hill and he settled in for the winter. Fabius also made camp, so until the spring of 216 B.C., the two armies watched each other from a distance.

THE BATTLE OF CANNAE

Hannibal moved his army as warmer weather returned. He had no choice. The storehouse of food was gone. His army had gathered everything available from the surrounding area. While the Romans had supplies delivered regularly to their camp, the Carthaginian resources had run out. Hannibal broke camp and marched south to Cannae. The Romans had a grain depot in the town. He planned to capture it. This served two purposes. The grain would provide food for Hannibal's warriors. It would also rob the Romans of a handy food supply.

Two new Roman consuls, Lucius Aemilius Paullus and Gaius Terentius Varro, were appointed in 216 B.C. Their legions were added to those already in the field. The Romans probably had eighty thousand foot soldiers and six thousand cavalry. Historians disagree on the exact number. The Carthaginian army was smaller. Hannibal had about forty thousand warriors.

The Roman consuls were keeping an eye on Hannibal. They marched to meet him at Cannae.[1] This year, the consuls did not divide the legions into two separate armies. They shared command in an unusual way. One consul commanded all the legions one day, and the other took charge the next. The command shifted back and forth daily. This arrangement created problems because the two consuls disagreed about when and where to attack Hannibal.[2] Paullus was cautious but Varro was ready for action.

Hannibal arrived in Cannae before the Romans. He scouted the territory. When he learned that the enemy was approaching, he set up camp. He picked a spot that was flat and suitable for a cavalry attack. The Romans stopped a few miles away, facing Hannibal. They settled in two sites on the east and west bank of the river that flowed through the plain.

A ROMAN VICTORY

As the Romans made camp, a minor skirmish took place. Hannibal's light cavalry attacked, but the legions drove them off. The Romans lost fewer than a hundred men. Seventeen hundred Carthaginians died. Varro claimed a victory. The following day, Paullus decided not to pursue their enemy because he feared a trap. Varro was furious.[3]

Though Hannibal had lost the first fight, he was not worried.[4] He considered it a test. Now he was confident that he could draw Varro into battle when he was ready. It was time to set another trap.

The next night Hannibal led his men out of camp. They took only their weapons. Everything of value was left behind. He hid his army behind nearby hills. They were lined up and ready for battle. Hannibal waited for the enemy to discover his deserted camp. When they moved in to collect the plunder, he planned to attack.

At dawn, Roman scouts moved closer to Hannibal's camp. They discovered it was deserted and rushed back to headquarters. They reported that the enemy had fled, leaving their tents standing and fires burning. The soldiers wanted to loot the area immediately. Paullus sent a small band of cavalry to scout the situation. They returned, reporting that it must be a trap. This news did not stop Varro. He led troops toward the Carthaginian camp. It was only by chance he avoided disaster. Two Roman slaves had escaped from Hannibal's force. They met up with Varro and reported that the Carthaginian army was on the other side of the hills, waiting to attack. The consul ordered a retreat.

The Battle Line Is Drawn

As Hannibal planned his next assault, trouble broke out in the Roman camp. The consuls could not agree on what to do. Paullus was in command that day. He refused to attack the Carthaginians. Meanwhile, Hannibal sent a small band of cavalry to harass the enemy. They attacked Romans collecting water from the river, and chased them nearly back to camp.

The next morning, Hannibal advanced with his foot soldiers and then followed with the rest of his army. The Carthaginians lined up facing north. Varro did not consult Paullus. He marched to meet Hannibal. Paullus followed, though he thought this was a mistake.[5]

An observer might have had trouble telling the two armies apart that day. Many Carthaginian warriors looked like Roman soldiers. Their weapons and armor had been part of the spoils from the Battle of Lake Trasimeno.[6]

The Romans lined up for battle facing south. A wind had come up. It carried clouds of dust into their eyes. The battle cry rang out and the cavalries charged. With the river on one side and a huge infantry force on the other, the riders had little space to maneuver. They were forced to charge head-to-head. The horses soon came to a complete stand still, jammed closely together. The mounted warriors dragged each other from the saddle. It was a fierce battle. The Roman cavalry was outnumbered by Hannibal's force. They soon gave up and retreated.

For a time, the infantries seemed evenly matched. Then the Romans began to make headway. The center of Hannibal's line began to collapse. Carthaginian warriors pulled back, drawing the Romans after them. This was exactly what Hannibal wanted. He had set another trap. The Romans continued to press forward. They paid no attention to Hannibal's second line of infantry. He had experienced warriors waiting on the sidelines. The legions continued to advance. Finally, they passed beyond Hannibal's troops waiting on each flank. Then he ordered his second line into battle. The Africans lowered their pikes and closed in, surrounding the Romans. This time the fight was not equal. The tired Romans were no match against a fresh force.

Paullus was seriously wounded by a stone from a slingshot, but he continued to ride back and forth

THE BATTLE OF CANNAE

1) The opposing cavalries clash.

2) Part of the Roman cavalry retreats as the Roman infantry meets the main line of Hannibal's infantry.

3) Carthage's cavalry drives away the remaining Roman cavalry. The main Carthaginian infantry falls back as Hannibal's reserve soldiers charge toward the advancing Roman army from the sidelines.

4) The Carthaginian cavalry advances to help Hannibal's infantry defeat the Romans.

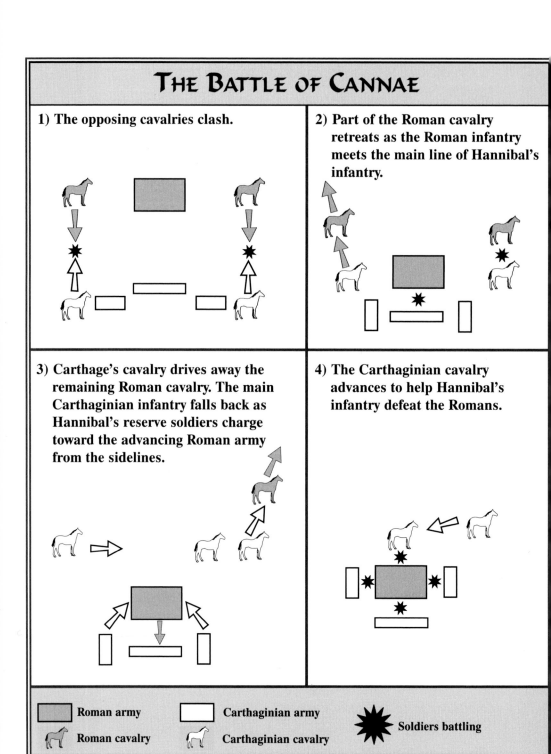

Roman army   Carthaginian army   Soldiers battling

Roman cavalry   Carthaginian cavalry

encouraging his men to keep fighting. He finally grew too weak to control his horse and had to dismount. One soldier recalled seeing the consul sitting on a rock, bleeding.[7] The Romans fought on and most made no attempt to escape. They preferred to die where they stood.[8] When the fighting ended, Hannibal had won another victory in what became known in history as the Battle of Cannae.

AFTER THE BATTLE

Hannibal sent his cavalry to round up fugitives. The consul Varro escaped with about seventy horsemen. Paullus died on the battlefield. The total number of Roman casualties was forty-five thousand infantry and twenty-seven thousand cavalry. Hannibal lost only eight thousand warriors.

Hannibal set Roman allies free as he had done after his summer victories. This time, he addressed his Roman prisoners. He told them he was not engaged in a war to the death with Rome. Hannibal then offered the Romans a chance to ransom themselves. They accepted his terms and a delegation went to Rome. Every Roman believed that Hannibal would now attack the city. They feared he would win one final victory.

Most of the Carthaginian officers now urged Hannibal to rest and to allow his troops to do the same. Only one disagreed. Maharbal was the commander of the Carthaginian cavalry. He believed that it was time to strike Rome. Livy recorded what he may have said to Hannibal: "Sir, if you want to know the true significance of this battle, let me tell you that within five days you will take your dinner, in triumph, on the Capitol. I will go first with my horsemen. The first knowledge of our coming will be the sight of us at the gates of Rome. You have but to follow."[9]

HANNIBAL'S NEXT MOVE

After the Battle of Cannae, Rome's allies began to waiver. Many decided to support Carthage instead. Hannibal wanted to secure these new territories

MAGO REPORTS TO CARTHAGE

Later that summer, Hannibal's brother Mago sailed to Carthage. He took news of the Battle of Cannae. He reported that his brother had defeated the Romans many times during the last three years. The Carthaginians had killed more than two hundred thousand in battle. They had taken more than fifty thousand prisoners. Then Mago poured gold rings taken from the enemy onto the courtyard. The rings created a dazzling heap.

Mago reminded the Senate, the governing body of Carthage, that Hannibal was fighting in enemy territory. He was far from home. He needed money to pay troops who had served Carthage so well. He needed grain for food. Warriors were also needed to reinforce the troops.

The Senate agreed to send four thousand cavalry, forty elephants, and a large sum of silver. Unfortunately, they saw no need to rush to Hannibal's aid. Much time would pass before the supplies and men reached Italy.

instead of marching to Rome. He divided his army in two. His brother Mago was ordered to control towns along the eastern coast.

Hannibal still needed a seaport. He marched to Naples on the southern coast of Italy. He planned to attack the city until he saw its strong walls. The general decided it could not be taken. He moved his army inland to Capua. The citizens of this town signed a pact with him. Hannibal now controlled another piece of Italy, but only for a short time before the Romans surrounded the city. The Carthaginians held on until more legions arrived. Then Hannibal was forced to withdraw.

For the rest of the summer, Hannibal moved about. He searched the western coast of southern Italy for a seaport. A port would make it possible for ships to cross safely from Carthage. He needed reinforcements and supplies the Senate had promised. The year 216 B.C. was a high point in Hannibal's war.[10] It also held the major disappointment that no port turned against Rome and the Carthaginian army failed to take one by force.

9

WAR IN ITALY AND ABROAD

The war between Carthage and Rome attracted much attention around the ancient world. Macedonia, a neighboring country separated from Italy by the Ionian Sea, watched events with special interest. Hannibal's victories over the Romans impressed King Philip V of Macedonia.[1]

In 215 B.C., Philip of Macedonia sent envoys to meet with Hannibal and negotiate a pact. The party landed in southern Italy. They traveled north and west toward Hannibal's camp. They avoided towns loyal to Rome but were stopped by a Roman patrol. When questioned, the envoys said King Philip had sent them to arrange a pact of friendship between Macedonia and Rome. Needing allies, the Romans welcomed the party from Macedonia and an agreement was quickly reached. The envoys were given a military escort to see them safely back to their ship. The Macedonians slipped away from the guards. They still planned to complete the job King Philip had sent them to do. They managed to make their way to the Carthaginian camp.

An Ally for Hannibal

Hannibal welcomed the Macedonians. Together they worked out a treaty. The terms were recorded by Livy, the Roman historian. He stated that King Philip

> was to cross to Italy with the largest fleet he could raise (perhaps two hundred ships) harry [attack] the coast, and carry on offensive operations by land and sea to the best of his ability; at the end of the war, Rome and all Italy were to pass into the hands of Hannibal and the Carthaginians, and all captured material was to be ceded to Hannibal. Italy once crushed, the Carthaginians were to sail for Greece and make war upon any states the king might choose.[2]

As soon as the treaty was ready, the Macedonian envoys sailed for home. They took three of Hannibal's officers with them. These men were to present the document to Philip V. They would then sign it on behalf of Carthage. Unfortunately, they did not reach the King. After leaving port, the Macedonian ship was stopped by the Roman navy. They searched the ship. They were suspicious of clothing worn by Hannibal's men. Then they found the treaty. Everyone was taken to Rome and thrown in jail.

Hannibal needed the Macedonian army and fleet. Many of Rome's allies would have come over to the Carthaginian side if King Philip had joined him. The envoy's capture was a serious setback.

REINFORCEMENTS ARRIVE

In the spring of 215 B.C., Hannibal's situation improved. Troops, elephants, and supplies finally arrived from Carthage. They avoided the Roman fleet. The ships landed at Locri, a Greek trading center near the southern tip of Italy. Locri had pledged allegiance to Hannibal after hearing of his daring victory at the Battle of Cannae. The troops marched north to join Hannibal. On the way, they ran into a force led by the consul Longus. The Romans got the best of the Africans during the skirmish. They killed two thousand warriors. They forced the Carthaginians to retreat. This battle showed that Roman war tactics were getting better.[3]

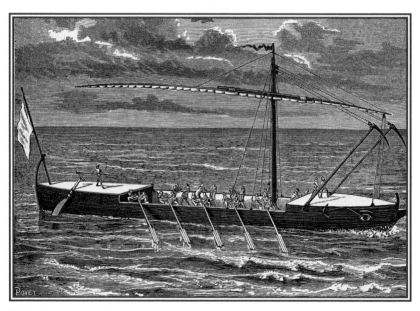

This Roman galley was called a quinquireme. Modern historians think that galleys were named based on the number of rows of men with oars. "Quin" means five; so, a quinquireme had five rows of men with oars. This type of ship was used against Carthage during the Punic wars.

The reinforcements finally reached the Carthaginian camp. Hannibal planned to blockade the walled seaport of Nola. As his warriors surrounded the town, the Romans saw an opportunity to launch a surprise attack on Hannibal. The legions lined up inside the town gate. When the time was right, they charged out, surprising the Carthaginians. The fighting was savage, but rain and a hailstorm ended the battle.

This small victory encouraged the Romans. The next day, they marched out of the walled port. They lined up for battle. Hannibal accepted the challenge, and the Romans quickly overpowered his troops. He was forced to retreat to camp. During the battle, five thousand Carthaginians were killed. Six hundred were taken prisoner. Many more were wounded. Hannibal also lost six elephants. He decided to end his summer fighting season and marched east to camp for the winter.

SPRING OF 214 B.C.

By the spring of 214 B.C., Rome was ready to fight again. They had eighteen legions in the field. These included two new legions to defend Rome. Work was also about to begin on a fleet of one hundred fifty ships.

Hannibal's allies in southern Italy watched Rome's growing might. They saw themselves as the prime target and asked Hannibal for protection. The Carthaginians, still in winter quarters, broke camp and marched at once. Within a few days, Hannibal reoccupied his camp near Capua, an important city in the territory he controlled. Though he held the coastal town of Locri, he was still having trouble receiving supplies and reinforcements. He left part of his army on guard while he set out in search of another seaport.

That summer, Hannibal marched from one coastal town to the next. As his army moved through the countryside, his warriors ransacked villages. They left fields planted with crops in ruins, but no seaport opened its gates to the Carthaginians.

Meanwhile, the two Roman consuls had joined forces. They marched across southern Italy. Settlements

TROUBLES IN ENEMY TERRITORY

Many difficulties Hannibal faced were due to the fact he was fighting in enemy territory. He was constantly searching for a dependable source of supplies. His army had to rely on allies for provisions, or on what they could forage from the land. Hannibal still only had the seaport of Locri. Unfortunately for him, the Romans knew that he needed another seaport. They reinforced these ports against attack.

Manpower was also a problem for Hannibal. He had gained control of a large area in southern Italy. Now he had to defend it. When he marched off in search of a seaport, he had to leave some troops behind. His army was not large enough to divide into several divisions. Splitting his forces made him an easy target for the Roman legions. Hannibal waited for more reinforcements. He hoped his brother Hasdrubal would arrive soon from Spain. He needed his help fighting in Italy.[4]

that had switched their support to Carthage were recaptured. The Romans punished the people who had turned against them. Crops were burned. Cattle were driven off, and men taken prisoner.

FALL OF TARENTUM

In 213 B.C., Hannibal again tried to capture a seaport. This time he turned his attention to Tarentum. It was located on the southern coast of the Italian peninsula. A Roman garrison guarded the town. They held several citizens hostage to ensure the local people would remain loyal. A few hostages escaped from the city. They were quickly recaptured. As punishment, they were whipped and then thrown off the cliffs to their death. The town's people resented this harsh treatment. They wanted to be free from Roman rule. The people sent a party of young men to Hannibal. Together, they worked out a plan to help him capture the city.

The young men agreed to leave the city nightly, pretending to go out hunting. They would come and go from the same gate, setting a pattern. The guards on duty would get in the habit of opening the gate when the hunting party signaled its return. Hannibal waited until he was certain the Romans had relaxed their guard. Then he marched toward Tarentum with ten thousand troops. He sent his cavalry in advance. They were to pretend to be a raiding party. He ordered them to seize or kill anyone who might catch a glimpse of his main fighting force.

When he was about fifteen miles from the city, the Roman historian Livy recorded that Hannibal "halted on the banks of a river . . . which offered excellent cover. There they enjoyed an evening meal and he briefed his officers. Even then he did not explain the details of his plan but dwelt on three points." First, he asked " . . . that they fight bravely, since the prize for success had never been greater." He also told them to keep their men marching in close order. They were to punish any who stepped out of line. Finally, "they were to carry out his orders to the letter and not attempt anything on their own."[5]

As soon as it was dark, Hannibal marched on. He made his way to the gate that the hunting party used repeatedly, signaling to be let in. The guards were expecting the party of hunters to return. They opened the gate and were quickly killed. Hannibal then led a party of thirty Carthaginians to the main gate. They forced it open so that the rest of the army could pour in. The town surrendered quickly. Many Roman troops were killed, but about five thousand escaped to a fortress on a rocky point near the harbor. Hannibal had gained a seaport, but while Romans held the fortress, ships could not sail in and out of the harbor without fear of attack.

THE FORTRESS OF TARENTUM

Hannibal tried to take the fortress near Tarentum by storm. He now had weapons for a siege. They had probably arrived from Carthage with his reinforcements. He used siege towers, catapults, and a variety of artillery,

Battles Across the Carthaginian Empire

While Hannibal tried to hold on in Italy, battles were being fought in other parts of the ancient world. Carthage tried to reclaim territory in Sicily with little success. The Roman fleet still controlled the Mediterranean Sea. They landed a legion near Carthage and their soldiers raided the countryside.

In Spain, the Romans continued to take territory south of the Ebro River. And in 213 B.C., they drove the Carthaginians from Saguntum. A battle for this city had started Hannibal's war campaign.

but the Roman troops remained safe inside the stronghold. Hannibal abandoned his siege when Roman reinforcements arrived by sea.

Hannibal soon came up with another plan to get ships out of the inner harbor. There were several roads between the docks and the town. He had the ships lifted from the water and placed upon wagons. The ships were then hauled through the town by men and mules to the sea on the far side. His plan worked. In a few days, the fleet sailed around the fortress and anchored in the mouth of the harbor. Hannibal believed this blockade would prevent more reinforcements and supplies from reaching the Roman troops holed up inside.[6]

Rome knew it was important to hold the fortress. It kept Hannibal from using the city's port. However, there was a real danger that their troops would starve. They sent a fleet loaded with grain to Tarentum. Somehow, the ships slipped through the Carthaginian patrols and landed safely. This was a crucial mistake because now the troops inside had plenty of food. The Carthaginians still had the fortress surrounded, but there was little hope that the Romans could be forced to surrender.[7]

Hannibal prepared to camp for the winter. His prospects looked gloomy. The Romans were reclaiming more and more territory. He still had no seaport. He had no reliable supply and communication line with Carthage. All he could do was wait. He needed reinforcements from Africa or Spain. The size of his army was shrinking. Even so, Hannibal refused to give up.[8]

CARTHAGE LOSES GROUND

In 210 B.C., Hannibal learned that a village in Italy under his rule was negotiating with the Romans. He moved quickly. His army approached the town ready for battle. Again the Roman legion was no match for his force. The consul and most of his warriors were killed. Only three thousand escaped. Hannibal dealt harshly with the townspeople. They had not remained loyal to him. He killed the men who tried to negotiate with Rome, then burned the town to the ground. This was his only victory that summer in Italy. Rome continued to take back territory it had lost to the Carthaginians.

BATTLE FOR SPAIN

Carthage also lost ground in Spain. This was due largely to the efforts of one young Roman. At the age of twenty-four, Publius Cornelius Scipio took command in Spain.

He had sailed there with a fleet of thirty vessels. The ships carried ten thousand infantry and one thousand cavalry troops.

When Scipio landed in Spain, he immediately sent out scouts. He wanted to know the whereabouts of the Carthaginian armies. He learned the enemy's forces were scattered about the country. All were at least a ten-day march from New Carthage, their capital city. His officers wanted to attack one of the armies but Scipio had a different idea. He planned to strike New Carthage. He spent the winter gathering information about the city. Scipio discovered it sat in a prime location on the coast of Spain. The site made it easy for Carthaginians to sail to and from Africa. It had a large harbor that merchant and navy fleets could use.

He discovered that huge amounts of money were stored in the city. Most of the Carthaginian army's weapons, uniforms, and equipment were there, too. Spanish hostages were held inside the walls. Scipio also learned one more important detail: Only one thousand troops guarded the city.

FATHER AND SON

Publius Cornelius Scipio was the son of a Roman consul. His father had met Hannibal at the Ticino River. That was the first battle Hannibal fought in Italy. During the fighting, the seventeen-year-old led a cavalry charge and helped save his father's life.

Next, Scipio gathered information about the area around New Carthage. The walled city sat on a lagoon. The lagoon was about two and one-half miles long and a mile wide. The opening to the sea was partially blocked by an island. This created a well-protected harbor. The city itself was built on a peninsula that stuck out into the lagoon. Water protected it on three sides. Scipio talked to local fishermen. He learned that the lagoon was shallow and at low tide it could be forded easily in many places by his men.

The young general now had a plan. He ordered his fleet to sail for New Carthage and blockade the lagoon. He marched south with his army and camped outside the city walls. Before he attacked, Scipio spoke to his troops. According to Livy, he reminded them that they were about to strike "the walls of one town, [and] in that one town you will have taken the whole of Spain."[1] He then ordered two thousand soldiers with ladders to advance to the walls of the city. His fleet closed in from the sea, firing missiles such as spears, stones, and objects that were on fire.

The commander inside the capital fought back. His troops marched from behind the city walls to meet the enemy. They were outnumbered by the Roman forces and soon turned and ran. Many Carthaginians were killed on the battlefield. More died trying to get safely back inside the city gates.

After this first assault, Scipio pulled back. He rested his warriors and planned his next attack. He ordered five hundred men to the water's edge. When he got word that the tide was low, Scipio sent troops to strike the front wall of the city. This drew the defenders' attention away from the lagoon.

Meanwhile, Scipio's men waded through the shallow water. They found the walls on the lagoon side unguarded and climbed over. The Romans made their way through the city, and opened the main gate. Scipio's army poured into New Carthage. They had orders to kill every man, woman, child, and beast. Nothing was to be left alive. The Carthaginians were completely outnumbered and they surrendered.

Scipio had won quite a prize. He sent news of the victory to Rome by ship. In addition to the city itself, he had captured a huge quantity of war materials. Livy recorded a detailed list:

> 120 catapults of the largest sort, 281 smaller ones; 23 large and 52 smaller ballistae [another kind of catapult]; countless scorpion catapults, large and small, and a great quantity of equipment and missiles, and, finally, 74 military standards [battle flags]. In addition much gold and silver was brought to Scipio; it included 276 gold platters, each being a pound in weight; 18,300 pounds of silver, either coined or in ingots; and a great many silver vessels. All this was handed over, weighed and measured. There were 400,000 measures of wheat and 270,000 measures of barley; 63 merchant vessels, some with their cargoes of grain and arms, besides bronze, iron, sail cloth, esparto [a tough wiry grass from North Africa] for rope making and timber for ship building.[2]

The following spring, Scipio attacked the Carthaginian army. Hannibal's brother Hasdrubal Barca was in command. The Romans surprised him. They surrounded his warriors before he could organize a defense. During the battle, eight thousand Carthaginians were killed. Twelve thousand were taken prisoner. Hasdrubal managed to escape. He marched over the Pyrenees into Gaul with the rest of his troops. A year later, Hasdrubal decided to go to Italy. He planned to join Hannibal and leave Scipio far behind in Spain.

The War in Italy

New Roman consuls were elected in the year 209 B.C. They were determined to recapture Tarentum.[3] One consul planned to keep Hannibal busy fighting while the other attacked the seaport. They had help from a traitor inside the city walls.

News reached Hannibal that Tarentum was under attack. He set out immediately to defend the city. He marched night and day but was still three miles away when he learned that the city was lost. The Romans had won the battle.

The following year, Hannibal set up camp near the two Roman consuls. He saw an ambush site on a wooded hill. After dark, the Carthaginian general sent part of his cavalry to hide among the trees. They stopped near the top of the hill.

Meanwhile, many officers in the Roman camps were worried about the same high ground. It overlooked their camps. They believed their troops should be stationed on that wooded hill. The two consuls decided to ride out together. They wanted to personally scout the area.

A Traitor Inside Tarentum

Love may have brought down the walls of Tarentum. According to one story, a captain stationed inside was desperately in love. The woman he loved had a brother serving in the Roman force attacking the city. The woman told her brother of her love. The brother told the consul. With the consul's approval, the woman's brother slipped into the city. He talked the lovesick captain into helping the Romans capture Tarentum. The captain agreed to let the Romans slip over the section of wall he was supposed to defend. The plan worked: The Romans climbed the city wall and opened the gates for the rest of the troops.

According to Roman historian Livy, when Hannibal learned how the Romans used treachery to take the city, he said, "The Romans, too, have their Hannibal; we have lost Tarentum by the same strategy as won it for us."[4]

After seeing the hill for themselves, they would decide what to do.[5]

Hannibal's warriors were already hiding on the hill. They watched as the consuls left camp with two cavalry squadrons. All the Carthaginians had to do was wait. The Romans rode into their trap. One consul was immediately run through with a lance and killed. The second consul was fatally wounded. The rest of the Roman troops retreated quickly. Hannibal had won one more victory, but continued to lose ground. Still he refused to leave Italy and return to his homeland.[6]

HASDRUBAL MARCHES TO ITALY

Reinforcements were on the way. Hasdrubal Barca marched towards Italy. He arrived in the Po Valley in the spring of 207 B.C. He sent a message to his brother Hannibal, including details of his route. He also suggested a place for their two armies to meet. Hasdrubal sent the message with a scouting party. The party rode most of the way down the Italian peninsula, trailing Hannibal. As they neared Tarentum, the scouts took a wrong turn. They were captured by Romans. Under threat of torture, the messengers revealed Hasdrubal's plans.

The consul Gaius Claudius Nero immediately sent word to Rome. Then he marched north. He planned to reinforce Roman forces waiting to confront Hasdrubal. He left part of his army in southern Italy. Their orders were to keep Hannibal occupied. Nero did not want him to join forces with his brother. The full force of the Roman legions was now directed at the reinforcements from Spain.

Hasdrubal marched south to meet Hannibal in 207 B.C. His scouts reported that the armies of two consuls blocked their way. Hasdrubal decided not to attack such a large force. He ordered all campfires put out. After dark, his army packed up. They retreated north. Unfortunately, the territory was unfamiliar. They lost their way in the dark.[7]

The next day, the Roman legions caught up with Hasdrubal and attacked. The battle lasted all morning. The Carthaginians were worn out from marching through the night. They suffered heavy losses and Hasdrubal was among those killed. When the battle ended, the Romans had won.

Nero returned to southern Italy quickly. He took Hasdrubal's head with him. He had it flung into the enemy camp. It was carried to Hannibal. The consul also released two Carthaginian prisoners. They gave Hannibal a full account of the battle. The news of his brother's death greatly distressed Hannibal. The historian Livy expressed Hannibal's feelings: "Now, at last, I see the destiny of Carthage plain!"[8]

Hannibal now had no hope of reinforcements. He collected what was left of his army. They marched south nearly to the very tip of the Italian peninsula. There they settled in for the winter. The Roman legions did not pursue Hannibal. They left him alone for a whole year after Hasdrubal's death. Livy wrote, that by the end of 207 B.C., it was clear that any hope for future Carthaginian victories was tumbling into ruin.[9]

CARTHAGE'S LAST BATTLES IN EUROPE

During 206 B.C., little fighting took place in Italy. But an important battle was fought in Spain. Hasdrubal Gisco, another Carthaginian general, was determined to regain territory lost to Rome. He raised an army of fifty thousand foot soldiers and forty-five hundred calvary. With this army, he set up camp in open country. He prepared to defend his position in southern Spain against the Roman legions.

Scipio soon got word of this new enemy force. He realized that his legion alone was no match for the Carthaginians. He needed to add Spanish allies to increase his numbers, but he did not want too many of these troops. He feared if the battle seemed to be going in favor of his enemy, troops from Spain might desert to the other side. That could turn the tide of a battle.[1]

Scipio raised a force of forty-five thousand. His legions included experienced Roman warriors and Spanish allies. They marched across Spain to do battle again with the enemy. When he drew near the Carthaginians, Scipio ordered his legions to halt. He built a fortified camp. As they were getting their defenses in place, Hasdrubal Gisco sent a cavalry squadron to attack the Roman workers. For awhile, it looked like the clever Carthaginians would win this first skirmish with Scipio in Spain.

Scipio expected something like this. He had part of his cavalry hidden behind a hill near the campsite. They swooped down in a counterattack. The first Carthaginian riders scattered quickly, but more warriors followed. They were determined to give battle. For awhile, both sides held their ground, but Scipio sent more and more reinforcements. The stronger Roman force soon overpowered the Carthaginians. They began pulling back. The retreat was orderly at first, but the Romans continued to attack. The Carthaginians soon broke and ran. Warriors rushed wildly back to camp, trying to escape with their lives.

Hasdrubal Gisco had lost this skirmish, but felt certain his whole army was strong enough to defeat the Romans. He lined up his main force for battle shortly after dawn the next day. The elephants were positioned in front.

Scipio also lined up his forces. Both armies stood, ready and waiting, but no one made a move. Near sunset, the Carthaginians and the Romans marched back into their camps. This standoff was repeated for several days.

Neither side advanced. No missile was thrown. No battle cry given. Each morning, the Carthaginian commander took the field first. Near dark, he was the first to withdraw. His warriors were tired of doing nothing.[2]

Scipio finally decided it was time to fight. He planned to surprise the Carthaginians by changing the pattern of events.[3] He ordered his men to eat a hearty meal before dawn. The horses were fed and groomed. Then he sent all his cavalry and light troops to attack the Carthaginian outposts. The Roman general followed with the rest of his troops.

Hasdrubal Gisco heard the Roman cavalry's battle cries. He rushed from his tent. His warriors raced for their weapons as Scipio's army advanced quickly. The Carthaginian general ordered his cavalry to advance. Then he led his infantry to meet the enemy.

For a time it was hard to tell which side was winning or losing. Then Scipio attacked in full force. It was soon clear that the Romans had an advantage. They were winning on every part of the field.

The battle raged on through the morning. Hasdrubal Gisco's men tired. They had been surprised by the Romans. There had been no time for food before the fighting began. By midday, they were hot, hungry, and thirsty. Many were so exhausted they had to lean on their shields for support. The frightened elephants milled about in the middle of the battlefield, adding to the confusion.

The Carthaginians sounded retreat. They fled back to camp with the enemy on their heels. The Romans continued to attack, pursuing them to the edge of their

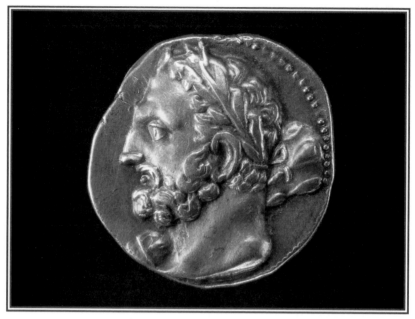

This coin was minted during the time of Hannibal. It shows the likeness of the Carthaginian god Melqart. Melqart was originally the Phoenician god of the sun.

camp. A rainstorm ended the battle. It saved what was left of Hasdrubal Gisco's army. The Romans made their way back to their own camp through the downpour.

The next day, the Carthaginians collected stones. They built up the walls around their camp. Many troops deserted. By this time, Hasdrubal saw only one way to escape. He packed up and moved during the night.

At dawn, Roman guards reported the enemy's camp was deserted. Scipio sent his cavalry after them, and then ordered his infantry to march. The Romans moved quickly and would have overtaken the Carthaginians if they had followed their trail. Instead Scipio took the advice of his guides. They claimed to know a shortcut to a ford. They believed the Carthaginians would cross a river there. It was a good spot for an ambush.

Scouts warned Hasdrubal Gisco that Scipio was waiting at the crossing. He took another route toward the coast. He hurried to put distance between his men and the Roman legions. The Carthaginian general escaped to the hills with about six thousand men. The rest of his force had been captured or killed. When they neared the coast, Hasdrubal Gisco sent for ships. He abandoned his men and escaped by night. No organized Carthaginian force was left in Spain. Scipio had won an important victory for Rome.

SCIPIO RETURNS TO ROME

Scipio was popular in Rome. He was elected consul in 205 B.C. The new consul wanted to take the war to Africa. He made plans for an attack on Carthage. Scipio spoke to the Roman Senate and asked them to approve his plans. The Senate assigned him to command the legions on the island of Sicily. They also gave him permission to sail to Africa. However, they only gave the consul thirty warships. This was not enough to carry all the troops he needed.

Scipio arrived in Sicily. He ordered his ships to raid the African coast. During these raids, Roman forces made contact with Masinissa. He was the ruler of Numidia, another country in Africa. Masinissa reported that the people of Carthage were growing tired of war.[4] Many of their allies were fighting local wars. They had to defend their own territory. These allies could not send

CARTHAGE LOSES AN ALLY

Numidian mounted warriors were an important part of the Carthaginian armies during the Second Punic War. At the beginning of the conflict, Masinissa, the country's ruler, supported Carthage. His warriors made up Hannibal's powerful cavalry. They helped him win many of the early battles.

In 206 B.C., Masinissa went over to the Roman side. Rome then used the Numidian cavalry against Carthage. In return, the Numidians gained control of more territory.

troops to help the African city. He urged Scipio to invade Carthage soon. Masinissa also agreed to send infantry and cavalry to fight alongside the Roman legions.

The Romans raided the Carthaginian coastline. Leaders in Carthage were alarmed and they feared Scipio would attack their city.[5] They decided to draw his attention to other battlefields. They sent a delegation to King Philip V of Macedonia. They asked him to invade Italy or Sicily. They offered a reward of two hundred talents. Other messengers were sent to Hannibal. They urged their general to do what he could to help. The Senate wanted him to stop the Romans before they attacked Carthage. These attempts did not work, and Scipio moved forward with plans to attack.

 ## THE SEAPORT OF LOCRI IS LOST

Scipio tangled once with Hannibal before sailing for Africa. He decided to drive the Carthaginians from

Locri. It was a seaport Hannibal controlled. Scipio got word to one of two garrisons in the port. He worked out a plan with its defenders. They agreed to hand the fort over to the Romans. Then, Scipio sent three thousand men to Locri.

When Hannibal heard this news, he marched to defend the port. Unfortunately, Scipio arrived first with his fleet. They hid troops inside the town. He laid a trap for the Carthaginian army. When Hannibal attacked, the Romans rushed out of the gates. They nearly surrounded his force. Hannibal had to withdraw quickly. Defeated, he marched away. It was the only important battle he fought in Italy in 205 B.C.

THE WAR GOES TO AFRICA

In the summer of 204 B.C., Scipio made an announcement. He would leave on the next fair wind. He thought this move would draw Hannibal from Italy. He wanted to take the war to Africa.

Scipio sailed for Africa with thirty thousand men and landed on the coast some distance from Carthage. The native people who lived in the area panicked.[6] They did not want to be caught in the middle of a battlefield. They packed up and moved inland, driving large herds of cattle.

Scipio needed a place for his base camp. He laid siege to the seaport of Utica. The city's defenses were too strong. He gave up after forty days. Scipio followed the coastline away from the city. He made camp for the winter near the sea. From this site, he could collect food from the countryside. He could also get supplies from Sicily and Italy. During the winter, he gathered information about the Carthaginian army.

Scipio studied the enemy camps. He learned that all their shelters were made of timber and dried reeds. These materials burned easily. He used this information to plan his first attack on his enemy. He sent troops to set fire to the camps. The flames spread quickly. The fire destroyed everything. Many Carthaginian warriors died. A few weeks later, Scipio lined up for full battle. He was ready to attack what was left of the Carthaginian armies in Africa. The battle did not last long and the Romans won easily. Hanno, Hannibal's brother, died defending his homeland.

Scipio then marched on Carthage. He camped about fifteen miles from the city. His army was visible from the capital. The Senate was certain that the Romans would attack soon. They sent a delegation to Scipio. They surrendered and asked to negotiate a treaty with Rome.

Scipio named his terms for peace. He demanded that Carthage hand over all prisoners of war and deserters. All but twenty warships had to be surrendered. Carthage had to give the Romans five hundred thousand measures of wheat and three hundred thousand of barley. In addition, they were to pay five thousand pounds of silver. There was one more important demand. Hannibal and his armies had to leave Italy.

The delegation had three days to make a decision. They quickly accepted Scipio's terms. The peace agreement was sent to Rome for approval.

LAST BATTLE IN ITALY

A year earlier, Mago Barca had landed in northern Italy with an army of fourteen thousand. Two Roman armies stood between him and Hannibal. He had not been able to reach his brother's camp.

Before the terms of the peace agreement reached Italy, Mago fought another battle with the Roman army. He was seriously wounded during the struggle. The loss of their commander shocked the Carthaginians.[7] They gave up the fight. Mago and his army retreated to the coast. He found messengers from Carthage waiting there. They ordered him to return to Carthage. The wounded commander set sail for home with his troops. He died at sea and Hannibal had lost his last brother.

Hannibal got orders to come home, too. Livy reported what he said when he received the message:

> For years past they have been trying to force me back by refusing me reinforcements and money; but now they recall me . . . in plain words. Hannibal has been conquered not by the Roman people whom he defeated in battle so many times and put to flight, but by the envy and disparagement [scorn] of the Carthaginian Senate.[8]

Hannibal prepared to sail but Carthage had sent no ships. He could only find enough vessels to transport his men. He had no space for his horses, so he had them killed.[9] He left Italy with twenty-four thousand men in the fall of 203 B.C., more than fifteen years after crossing the Alps.

12

WAR IN AFRICA

This was Hannibal's first time in his homeland since he had gone to Spain with his father at the age of nine. He was now forty-five years old. The general set up camp one hundred miles south of Carthage at Hadrumentum, near modern-day Sousse, Tunisia. Warriors from Mago's army joined him. They brought news of his brother's death. Hannibal rebuilt his army during the winter and waited for word that a peace agreement had been signed.

Before the signed treaty arrived, the peace was broken—the result of bad weather. A fleet of two hundred Roman transports loaded with supplies was caught in a storm. Blown off course, the ships were wrecked near Carthage. The people of the city salvaged great quantities of grain. They even towed some vessels back to the city.

Scipio was furious because he needed those supplies for his army.[1] He sent envoys to Carthage. They demanded that all the food stores be returned. Scipio also wanted the ships surrendered. He accused the Carthaginians of breaking the truce.

Members of the Carthaginian Senate were angered by Scipio's demands. They saw no reason to return the ships and supplies. They were more courageous now that Hannibal and his army were nearby.[2] They believed their general could defeat the Roman army. The Senate refused to return anything.

The envoys sailed back to Scipio empty-handed. When they cleared the mouth of the bay, they were attacked by three Carthaginian warships. The Roman sailors out-maneuvered the warships and made it back to Scipio. Most of the sailors on board were killed, but the envoys survived the ordeal.

AT WAR AGAIN

Rome and Carthage were at war again. The Romans held the Carthaginians responsible for breaking the truce and Scipio set out to punish Carthage. He attacked cities across the region, refusing to let them surrender. Taking each town by force, he sold the people into slavery.[3] He also sent messengers to Masinissa in Numidia. He asked him for reinforcements to fight beside his Roman legions.

The Carthaginian Senate begged Hannibal to stop the Romans. Hannibal told messengers he would choose the right moment to fight. The Carthaginian general knew his army was not ready for battle. He waited for cavalry reinforcements to arrive and he trained war elephants as best he could. However, they were young and had never been in a battle.

Hannibal moved his camp a few days later. He marched to Zama, a town about five days' journey southwest of Carthage. Next, he sent three spies to discover Scipio's whereabouts. These men were captured and taken to the Roman commander. Instead of torturing the spies, Scipio showed them about his camp. He gave them provisions and an escort. He instructed them to make a careful report to Hannibal of everything they had seen.

Hannibal was impressed by Scipio's boldness.[4] He decided the two should talk. He sent a messenger to the Roman camp. The consul agreed to a meeting and promised to send his own messenger, setting a time and a place.

Scipio waited for his ally Masinissa. He arrived with ten thousand warriors who set up camp closer to Hannibal. Scipio then picked a day and time to meet with his enemy.

On that day, Hannibal and Scipio rode out from their camps. They were escorted by a few horsemen. They met in private, with only interpreters there to hear what was said. The Greek historian Polybius recorded this account: Hannibal saluted Scipio and spoke first. He told the consul that he wished

> the Romans had never coveted [desired] any possessions outside Italy, nor the Carthaginians any outside Africa. Both peoples had built up noble empires, and Nature . . . had marked out their proper limits. 'But first of all we went to war to decide the possession of Sicily and afterwards that of Spain . . . we have reached the point at which one of us has risked the safety of his native soil in

the past, while the other is doing so at this moment . . . Today I am in Africa, on the point of negotiating with you, a Roman, concerning my country's very existence and my own.[5]

Hannibal ended by offering Rome all rights to the lands they were fighting over. He asked again for terms of peace from Scipio.

Scipio pointed out that Carthage had been the invader in the wars for Sicily and Spain. He reminded Hannibal that his city-state had again broken the peace by attacking his envoys. His ended with this statement: "You must put yourself and your country unconditionally into our hands, or else fight and conquer us."[6]

It seemed that no compromise could be reached by the two leaders. Hannibal and Scipio returned to their camps. The next morning both generals lined up their armies for battle.

THE BATTLE OF ZAMA

The Roman army was smaller in number than the Carthaginian force, but had two advantages. Scipio's troops were experienced Roman soldiers. In addition, Masinissa of Numidia, Hannibal's former ally, had arrived with cavalry support. These horsemen were considered the best in the world.

In the past, Hannibal's cavalry had won him great victories. This time he had few mounted warriors. He was forced to use elephants instead of horsemen for this battle. He placed all eighty elephants in front of his army. He hoped that they would smash the Roman front line and cause them to panic.

When the battle began, the elephants led the charge for Carthage. Hoping to scare their enemy into a retreat, their drivers encouraged the great beasts to trumpet. Instead, the Romans stood their ground. They sounded their own war trumpets and shouted loudly. The elephants were young with little training and they panicked. Some turned and stampeded into the front line of the Carthaginian army. Others crashed into the cavalry troops that formed Hannibal's left wing.

Livy described how the elephant charge ended:

> A few of the elephants, who had not panicked, did charge, and caused frightful execution [death] amongst the Roman velites [front line of foot soldiers] . . . the light troops, springing back . . . let the beasts through, . . . hurled their spears from right and left simultaneously, thus catching them in a cross-fire; the javelins of the front-line troops continued meanwhile to do their work, until under a hail of missiles from every side the elephants were driven out of the Roman line and, like the others, turned against their own men and even put to flight the Carthaginian cavalry on the right wing.[7]

Scipio ordered his Roman legions to advance. They drove the enemy's front line back into a second line of more experienced troops. The retreating warriors were not allowed to pass through the line. Spears of the next group of soldiers forced them toward the flanks. Many fled from the battlefield. The Roman cavalry galloped after those trying to escape.

For awhile, the two armies seemed evenly matched. Then Hannibal's second line fell apart. He moved in with his most experienced warriors that he had kept in reserve. The final action of the Battle of Zama was foot soldier against foot soldier. The two lines advanced and then retreated. The battlefield was covered with blood, dead bodies, and wounded men. Neither side could overpower the other. Finally, the scales tipped in Scipio's favor. His cavalry force returned to the battlefield after pursing the Carthaginian horsemen. These reinforcements were too much. Even Hannibal's best warriors gave up. The battle was over and the Romans had won.

Hannibal left the battlefield with a small escort. He made his way to Carthage to report his defeat and the end of the war.

THE END OF THE SECOND PUNIC WAR

Scipio again sent terms for peace. This agreement was presented to the Carthaginian Senate. Carthage could keep all the territory held in Africa before the war. They would be governed by their own laws. No Roman troops would stay in the city. Carthage had to pay damages. This covered acts of war committed during the truce. They had to hand over prisoners of war and their elephants. All warships except ten went to Rome. The city-state could not declare war on any people outside Africa. They could not attack other African countries without Rome's consent. The list of terms went on. Carthage was to supply the Roman army with enough grain for three months. They also had to give Rome ten thousand talents. This would be paid in installments over the next fifty years.

Rome did not demand that Hannibal be turned over to them as part of the peace treaty. The general was allowed to remain in Carthage. Some believe he was not taken captive because Scipio admired him.[8]

One senator rose to speak against the terms. Hannibal pulled him off the speaker's platform with his own hands. This angered others in the governing body.[9] Hannibal apologized. He said he had been away too long. He was unfamiliar with the Senate's rules. According to Polybius, the Greek historian, this is the speech Hannibal then made. As with all reports from this time, it may not be accurate.

> It seems to me amazing and indeed quite beyond my comprehension that anyone who is a citizen of Carthage and has full knowledge of the policies which we . . . adopted against Rome should not thank his stars that now that we are at their mercy we have obtained such lenient [easy] terms. If you had asked only a few days ago, what you expected your country would suffer in the event of a Roman victory, the disasters which threatened us then appeared so overwhelming that you would not even have been able to express your fears. So now I beg you not even to debate the question, but to declare your acceptance of the proposals unanimously, to offer up sacrifices to the gods, and to pray with one voice that the Roman people may ratify the treaty.[10]

There was no further debate and the Carthaginian Senate accepted the terms. Envoys were sent to Rome.

HANNIBAL'S LAST YEARS

The Second Punic War was over, but Hannibal still had a great deal of work to do. Still a military general, he was also given a new job as the chief magistrate of Carthage. The peace treaty required the city-state to pay damages to Rome. Carthage needed to regain its position as a wealthy trading nation. Its economy had to be rebuilt. It would take a strong leader to do that. Hannibal accepted the challenge. He was an honest and capable leader. He proved that he could lead his country in peacetime, as well as war.

One of the problems that Hannibal and the Senate faced was how to make the first payment to Rome for war damages. The council members discussed how to raise such a huge amount of silver on time. Hannibal laughed out loud at their worries. The Senate lectured him for taking the situation lightly. Hannibal told members that now was not the time to complain about their fate. If they had wanted to weep, it should have been when their arms and ships were taken from them.[1]

ROMAN WAR HERO RETURNS HOME

Scipio and his army returned home from Carthage after the peace agreement was signed. All of Rome's citizens welcomed the young general. His success in Africa had made him famous. Even his enemies honored him. He was responsible for winning the war against Carthage. It was a victory to celebrate. The streets were lined with flowers. Scipio rode at the head of his troops. They paraded through the city. African war elephants followed his army. The strange beasts amazed the people with their trumpeting. Scipio was also honored with a new name. From that time on he was known as Scipio Africanus. He was the first Roman consul to take a name from the country he conquered.[2]

REBUILDING CARTHAGE

For the next seven years, Hannibal worked to rebuild Carthage. Slowly it developed into an important trading nation again. He managed the city's money well and paid war damages each year. He also made certain that Carthage followed the terms of its peace agreement with the Roman Republic.

Whether or not Hannibal hoped to take revenge on his old enemy, no one knows for sure. As the country's leader in peace and war, he certainly realized how much Carthage had lost to Rome. The Carthaginians no longer held any lands in Spain. They had lost Sicily. They could not declare war without Rome's permission. Whatever his personal feelings, Hannibal did all he could to keep the peace.[3]

Even with all Hannibal accomplished, he had enemies in the city-state. Many Carthaginians blamed him for the Second Punic War. Plus, many Romans still considered him dangerous and they resented his accomplishments. In a very few years, Hannibal had rebuilt Carthage into a powerful trading nation. Both his enemies in Carthage and in Rome wanted him removed from the position of chief magistrate. The Romans petitioned their Senate to demand that Carthage remove Hannibal. Scipio got involved in the debate. He said that Rome had no right to meddle in Carthaginian affairs. He stopped them from interfering, but resentment toward Hannibal grew in Carthage and Rome.

TRAITOR!

In 200 B.C., war broke out between Rome and Macedonia. Three years later, Rome defeated King Philip V of Macedon. Philip was forced to give up his fleet and territory in Greece. He also had to pay a large sum for war damages. Roman leaders believed Hannibal had aided the Macedonians. This act violated the peace treaty that ended the Second Punic War.

Rome sent envoys to Carthage. They accused Hannibal of helping an enemy of Rome, and demanded his surrender. When Hannibal heard this, he feared his enemies in the Carthaginian Senate would hand him over.[4] He planned his escape.

Hannibal welcomed the Roman envoys and escorted them to their quarters in the city. During the day, he went about his business as usual. That night he pretended to go for a ride to enjoy the cool evening air. Instead, Hannibal galloped away from Carthage. He escaped to a house he owned along the Mediterranean Sea. A ship waited there for him. He loaded his belongings and sailed away with his entire fortune.

By the next morning, his enemies in Carthage realized they had been tricked. But it was too late. No one could catch Hannibal. He had too great a head start. The Roman envoys were furious.[5] Hannibal was declared an outlaw by the Senate. They seized property he had left behind and destroyed his house.

Escape

Hannibal's ship stopped at an island off the African coast. Other ships, on their way to Carthage, were tied up in the harbor. This made Hannibal uneasy. He did not want word of his whereabouts to reach people in his home city too quickly. Again, he came up with a plan. He invited the captains and crews of the nearby ships to dine with him on the island. He suggested they bring ashore the sails from their ships. The sails were strung up as awnings for protection against the hot sun. Hannibal entertained his guests all day and into the night. After everyone else fell asleep, he and his crew sailed away.

By the time his guests woke the next morning, Hannibal was gone. No one knew which direction he had sailed. It was too late to try to catch him. It would take far too long to rig up the sails. A few weeks later, Hannibal landed at Tyre in Phoenicia. This was the region from which the ancient founders of Carthage had come. He was welcomed by Antiochus, the ruler of Syria, and allowed to stay. For awhile, Hannibal lived safely in Tyre.

A few stories survive about Hannibal during his years of exile. Once he was invited by Antiochus to listen to a lecture. The speaker was an old teacher who specialized in military studies. After the lecture, when Hannibal was asked what he thought of the program, he remarked: "In my time I have listened to some old fools, but this one beats them all."[6]

HANNIBAL AND SCIPIO MEET AGAIN

While in Tyre, Hannibal suggested to Antiochus that the two of them attack Rome. He asked the king for an army of ten thousand foot soldiers. He also wanted one thousand horsemen and a fleet of one hundred ships. With this force, Hannibal would land in Italy while Antiochus would attack Greece.

Hannibal's plan was discovered by his enemies in Carthage. The information was intercepted when a man from Tyre visited the African city and contacted friends of Hannibal. Hannibal's enemies leaked the details to the Romans. The Romans sent a delegation to Antiochus. They wanted to know if he planned to help their enemy. Rome's intervention made Antiochus uneasy about assisting Hannibal.[7] He decided not to give the

Carthaginian general men and ships so he could return to Italy and fight again.

Scipio was the leader of the Roman envoys who questioned Antiochus. He also invited Hannibal to meet with him. Livy later wrote of the conversation that supposedly took place between the two men: After discussing old times, Scipio asked a question. He wanted to know who Hannibal thought was the greatest general in history.

"Alexander the Great," replied Hannibal.

"Whom do you put next?" inquired Scipio.

GENERALS IN EXILE

"At almost the same time, the two greatest cities of the ancient world acted ungratefully toward two of their leading citizens," Livy wrote, and he considered Rome to be the more ungrateful. "The conquered Carthage expelled [tossed out] the conquered Hannibal, but the victorious Rome drove out their victorious general Scipio Africanus."[8]

Not long after his second meeting with Hannibal, Scipio faced enemies of his own in Rome. He was accused by Cato, a member of the Roman Senate, of negotiating the peace treaty with Carthage to his own advantage. He also accused him of stealing public money. Scipio was called before a tribunal or a court. He came with papers that proved he was innocent, but refused to stay and defend himself. Instead, Scipio left Rome. He retired to his home in the Italian countryside near Linterno.

"Pyrrhus," replied Hannibal.

"Whom do you put next?" continued Scipio.

"Myself," said Hannibal.

Scipio laughed and continued, "What would you have said if you had beaten me?"

"I should have regarded myself as the greatest general of all," replied Hannibal. Scipio accepted this as a compliment.[9]

WAR BETWEEN ROME AND SYRIA

In 191 B.C., Rome ordered Antiochus of Syria to withdraw from all the Greek cities he held. He refused and Rome declared war. Antiochus divided his army, reserving most of his force to defend Syria and sending a smaller army to hold territories in Greece. The Romans defeated Antiochus in Greece and in Syria.

Hannibal felt certain that his freedom was at risk. He was sure Rome would demand his surrender as part of the peace agreement with Antiochus. Once again, he planned his escape. He left Syria and sailed for Crete, an island in the Mediterranean. It was the home of pirates. Few travelers stopped there. On the island, Hannibal faced a different kind of danger. The Cretans knew he had come with a great deal of money. To prevent his treasure from being stolen, Hannibal filled a number of narrow-necked jars almost to the top with lead. Then he covered the worthless material with a thin layer of gold pieces. He placed these heavy jars in a temple on the island, and asked the Cretans to guard them. Meanwhile,

Hannibal hid his real treasure in hollow bronze statues he left lying about in his garden.[10]

Unfortunately, even living on a remote island did not keep Hannibal out of danger. A Roman squadron visited Crete. They had orders to put the pirates out of business. They inspected the island's resources and harbors. The Romans had no idea that Hannibal lived on Crete. No one bothered him, but he realized it was only a matter of time before someone was sure to tell the Romans where he lived. Once again, Hannibal left secretly. He took all the statues from his garden with him.

DEATH

Hannibal moved to the kingdom of Bithynia in Asia Minor (in present-day Turkey). Bithynia was at war with Pergamum, another small kingdom under Rome's protection. Hannibal offered to help fight the war. Bithynia's army had been defeated on land, but fighting continued at sea. Hannibal advised the Bithynians to

THE DEATH OF SCIPIO AFRICANUS

Scipio Africanus died in 182 B.C. At the time, he was living in Italy on his estate far from the capital city. He refused to be buried in Rome. He left these instructions for the inscription on his tombstone. It was to read: "My ungrateful country shall not have my bones."[11] He never forgave Rome for the accusations made against him.

collect poisonous snakes. He told them to put the snakes in large jars and throw the jars onto enemy ships. The Bithynian sailors laughed at this suggestion, but tried it anyway. When the jars crashed on board the enemy ships, the poisonous snakes escaped. Soon, reptiles were crawling all over the decks. The enemy warriors quickly laid down their arms and surrendered.[12]

However, Rome came to Pergamum's aid and put a stop to the war. During the peace negotiations, they learned Hannibal had helped Bithynia. Rome demanded his surrender. The home Hannibal had built in Bithynia had seven exits. Some of the doors were hidden. He planned to always have a way to escape. This time his plan failed. Livy recorded what happened next. He wrote that the, "power of kings leaves nothing undiscovered

In 183 B.C., Hannibal took poison, preferring to die rather than be captured by the Romans.

when they wish to have it found out."[13] Hannibal learned soldiers were waiting for him at his front door. He tried escaping by a side door. It took only a few minutes to discover that every exit was guarded.

He realized there was no escape. He ordered a servant to bring him a draft of poison. Livy wrote that, as he drained the cup, Hannibal said, "Let us now put an end to the great anxiety of the Romans, who have thought it too lengthy, and too heavy a task, to wait for the death of a hated old man."[14] Hannibal died in 183 B.C. at the age of sixty-four.

THE THIRD PUNIC WAR

The Third Punic War began in 149 B.C., more than fifty years after the end of Hannibal's War. An uneasy peace had existed between Rome and Carthage for half a century. Carthage had made regular payments for war damages. They lived with the terms of the treaty agreed to in 201 B.C., even when their own territory was threatened.

One part of the peace agreement was particularly difficult for Carthage. Rome had rewarded Masinissa, the ruler of nearby Numidia who had helped defeat Carthage, with the right to claim lands that had belonged to his ancestors. That included nearly all the territory Carthage held. Only the city itself was excluded.[1]

For years, Masinissa seized more and more territory. Carthage could not fight back because they were not allowed to declare war without Rome's approval. Carthage asked Rome to stop Masinissa. But he continued to be a faithful ally of Rome. He sent men and provisions to wars in Spain, Macedonia, and Greece.

Because of this he continued to receive Rome's support in disputes with Carthage.

APPEALS TO ROME

In 152 B.C., Masinissa decided to seize even more Carthaginian territory, including rich farmlands. Again Carthage asked Rome for help. A delegation was sent from Rome to Africa. Cato was a member of the group. He was the Roman senator who had accused Scipio Africanus of illegal acts. The delegation traveled around the country. They saw fertile fields and wealthy people. In the city, they saw more signs of success. They realized Carthage was once again an important trading nation. This worried Cato and other members of the delegation. Carthage would make its last war payment the next year. They feared the city would no longer feel subject to Rome's control. Cato was convinced that if Carthage was not destroyed, it would destroy Rome.[2] The delegation refused to stop Masinissa. They returned to Rome and declared Carthage to be a serious threat.

During the next year, relations between Numidia and Carthage grew worse. Carthage asked Rome repeatedly for support. Rome continued to side with Masinissa. The Carthaginians finally lost their patience and invaded Numidia. This act broke the peace treaty of 201 B.C. Masinissa easily won the battle against the Carthaginian army. He brought news to Rome of Carthage breaking the treaty.

ROME DECLARES WAR

Rome was the most powerful country in the Mediterranean world. Even fifty years after the end of the Second Punic War, the Romans hated Carthage. Cato managed to fire up this hatred. The African city-state had almost destroyed them. He made sure its destruction became a goal for Rome. He felt strongly about this. He ended every speech, whatever its topic, with the phrase: "Carthage must be destroyed."[3] Rome declared war on Carthage in 149 B.C. The African city-state realized it had little hope of winning. Most of its army had been destroyed by Masinissa. The city was an easy target. Carthage sent a delegation to Rome. The Carthaginians surrendered without a fight. They promised to do whatever was required. They offered Rome all their territories and cities. That included the people, rivers, harbors, temples, and towns.

At first, the Roman Senate granted Carthage its freedom. The citizens were allowed to keep all their territories and possessions. They could follow their own laws. In return, Carthage had to send three hundred young men from noble families as hostages. Additional terms would be sent later.

The delegates returned to Carthage. One member of the Senate recalled no mention had been made of the city of Carthage itself. This made the leaders uneasy, but they followed instructions. Then they waited to hear the rest of Rome's terms.

Since Rome had declared war, its legions were already on their way to Africa. The consuls landed with eighty thousand foot soldiers and four thousand cavalry troops. They set up a base near the seaport of Utica, and arranged a meeting with the leaders of Carthage.

THE FINAL DEMAND

The Carthaginians met with the consuls. The entire Roman army looked on. The consuls first asked Carthage to hand over all arms. The delegation agreed. All weapons were sent to Utica. These included armor for two hundred thousand men, more spears and javelins than anyone could count, and two thousand catapults.[4] It seemed Carthage was disarmed.

After this, the consuls revealed the final terms: "Surrender Carthage to us, and retire anywhere you like within your own territory, so long as it is at least ten miles from the sea. We have decided to raze [to destroy] your city."[5]

The Carthaginians were shocked. A trading nation could not survive ten miles from the sea. They tried to reason with the consuls. They reminded them that Carthage had abided by the terms of the treaty made with Scipio Africanus. They had made war payments promptly. The city had also submitted to all of Rome's recent demands. Finally, they asked the consuls to think of Rome's reputation. How would the rest of the world view this act?

FORCED TO FIGHT

This final demand angered the citizens of Carthage. Members of the Senate who had supported Rome were attacked. Romans in the city were assaulted. The people crowded into the temples. They raged at the gods who had failed to help.[6] That same day, the Carthaginian Senate declared war on Rome.

The gates of the city were closed. Men, women, and children set to work. Metal cooking utensils, vessels, and statues were melted down. The people of Carthage toiled day and night to build shields, swords, missiles, spears, and javelins. Women cut off their hair and braided it into strings for catapults.

The Romans would now have to take Carthage by force. The city was protected by strong fortifications. Two lagoons, a great ditch, an earth wall, and a palisade protected it. That first summer, the Roman legions made three attacks on the city. Each time the people of Carthage drove them off. One consul decided to build battering rams. He had his troops collect timber. They made two of the weapons. One was so large it took six thousand men to move it. With these battering rams, the Romans broke through the city's walls. The Carthaginians worked all night, repairing most of the damage. They also destroyed the Roman battering rams.

ROMAN CONSUL SCIPIO AEMILIANUS

In 147 B.C., Scipio Aemilianus was elected Roman consul. He was the adopted grandson of Scipio Africanus. He arrived in Africa with reinforcements and took command of the legions. The Carthaginians prepared for a strong attack on the walls of their city. His army built a

127

fortified camp in front of the city, hoping to stop the Romans.

During Scipio's first attack, four thousand men broke through the city's defenses. They found themselves in an area of orchards, vineyards, and olive groves. The terrain was crisscrossed by irrigation canals. It was not a good place to fight, so Scipio withdrew. He camped on a spot where he could watch everything that happened inside the city. The boat docks were the only place hidden from his view.

Carthage continued to hold out. Food and provisions still reached them by sea, even through the Roman fleet's blockade. Scipio tried to cut off the supply route. He ordered his men to build a mole, or dam. It would block the waterway from the city's two harbors to the sea. The mole was made of stones piled one on top of the other. When it was finished it was twenty-four feet across at the top and ninety-six feet wide at the base. It was almost half a mile long.[7]

The Carthaginians had to find another way to get supplies. They built a new waterway. It went from the city's inner harbor to the sea. Everyone helped dig. Even the women and children pitched in. Others built ships inside the boatyard, hidden from the Romans' view.

Scipio was caught off guard when a new Punic fleet sailed down the channel and out to sea. The Romans had left their own fleet unattended while they built the mole. If the Punic fleet had attacked immediately, it would have destroyed their enemy's ships. Instead they waited three days. By that time, the Romans were ready for them. The battle ended as a draw.

It was now clear that Carthage had no chance of winning the war. Even so, the citizens refused to give up. They were still getting supplies and the siege continued during the winter. Scipio captured all the African towns loyal to Carthage. This finally stopped the flow of supplies to the capital. Carthage was now the only city left for Rome to conquer.

Later that winter, the Carthaginian general Hasdrubal asked for terms of peace. Scipio refused to show the city mercy. He did offer the general a way out. If he surrendered Carthage, Hasdrubal, his family, and ten friends would be allowed to live. The general refused the offer. He told Scipio that the finest funeral for men of spirit was to die in the flames of their native city.[8]

THE END OF THE SIEGE

Scipio's command was extended for another year. In the spring of 146 B.C., he attacked Carthage again. By the end of the first day, his warriors scaled the walls and advanced through the streets. The next day, the young consul moved up fresh troops who were faced with a difficult task. Hasdrubal and all the people had taken refuge in the city's fortress that sat at the top of a hill. Three streets lined with houses six or more stories tall climbed steeply to the fortress. Each had to be taken one by one. Those inside the buildings knew the situation was desperate. They fought in the streets and on the flat roofs, resisting to the end. Bodies fell from roofs and windows. This fierce battle lasted for six days. Scipio regularly called up fresh troops. He sent those who had been fighting back to camp, before they lost their nerve. Scipio did not sleep and stopped only briefly for food.

The rubble blocking the streets had to be cleared before soldiers could attack the city's last stronghold. Scipio ordered everything burned to the ground. Many had taken cover in secret hiding places in the houses and they died in the fires.

The Romans expected the battle to continue, but on the seventh day the citizens of Carthage surrendered. They asked only that their lives be spared. Scipio agreed. Fifty thousand men, women, and children gave up. They were placed under guard and later sold as slaves.

Hasdrubal, his wife and two children, and some nine hundred Roman deserters held out for awhile longer. Then Hasdrubal lost his will to fight. He begged for Scipio's mercy. Others preferred death to being captured by the Romans. They set fire to the stronghold. Hasdrubal's wife cursed her husband as a coward. She killed her two children then threw herself into the flames.[9] The siege of Carthage was over and Scipio Aemilianus had won a victory for Rome.

CARTHAGE DESTROYED

What was left of Carthage was set on fire. The fires burned for many days. It was reported that while Carthage burned, Scipio was moved to tears. Polybius, the Greek historian, witnessed this, and asked Scipio why he cried. Scipio replied, "O Polybius, it is a grand thing, but, I know not how, I feel a terror and dread, least some one should one day give the same order about my own native city."[10]

One story passed down through the years says that the Romans spread salt over the destroyed city of Carthage. This would keep anyone from rebuilding on the site because salt poisons plants people grow for food. No crops would grow there for years to come. Historians now question whether this actually happened.[11] What is known for sure is that Carthage and all its territory became the Roman Province of Africa—a small part of the Roman Empire.

CARTHAGE YIELDS TO ROME

When Rome burned Carthage to the ground, Hannibal had been dead for sixty years. Even then, what happened during his life continued to affect his African home. Romans had not forgotten the war with Hannibal.

The First and Second Punic wars changed Rome. The city started from humble beginnings. It was founded five hundred years before Hannibal's time. The people were farmers. They expanded when they needed more territory. They occupied the fertile lands of neighboring tribes. The first war with Carthage helped Rome became a sea power.

Then in 218 B.C., Hannibal invaded their lands. It took the Romans fifteen years to drive him out. The city-state grew more powerful during that time. They realized the value of colonies. Territories added to the resources of their homeland. Now, they wanted to expand.[1]

The war also changed Rome's armies.[2] The consuls followed Hannibal's example. They learned better war tactics and used these lessons well. They discovered how to beat Carthage and other enemies. They conquered new territories, adding lands in and around the Mediterranean.

The Second and Third Punic wars gave birth to an empire, according to Polybius, a Greek historian. He claimed Rome's growth began during those years. The city-state grew into a world power.[3] Rome occupied Spain, Sicily, and Sardinia. The Romans controlled parts of southern Gaul, Numidia, and much of Greece. They influenced other lands such as Egypt. They defeated three great rivals: Carthage, Macedonia, and Syria. They controlled the Mediterranean Sea.

HISTORY RECORDED

Carthage was destroyed, including all records, books, and documents. Thankfully, the historic events of that time were considered important. Records of the war were written down and saved, but the history of Carthage was retold by the enemies they fought. When the city burned, their culture was lost as was the Carthaginian point of view.

The Punic wars started a trend. These events led the Romans to begin writing the history of its people.[4] It was first recorded in Greek and then in Latin. Two authors did their best to preserve the details of the Punic Wars. Polybius was the earliest writer. He began his work soon after Carthage was destroyed in 146 B.C. He witnessed the Third Punic War. He also spoke with men who had fought in Hannibal's War. Polybius wrote forty volumes.

A Lost Culture

Phoenicians are said to have invented the alphabet. Carthage was founded by settlers from that country. These two nations disappeared long ago. What we know about them today was recorded by other cultures. These ancient people are interesting to study. However, first-hand data is scarce. Only a few written records survived.

Very little writing of the Carthaginians exists today. There are a handful of phrases recorded. One essay on farming was saved. All other written documents were lost. There is also very little known about the architecture and arts and crafts of Carthage.[5]

His history detailed the growth of the Roman Empire. It started at the beginning of the Punic wars. The author ended with the destruction of Carthage. Some of his writings survive. These volumes include his account of the war with Hannibal. He recorded the political and military events of the war. He discussed the causes and effects in a factual manner.[6] Polybius thought history had a purpose. He wrote to train leaders. He also wanted to teach citizens how to face disaster.

Livy, a Roman historian, also recorded the history of the Punic wars. He began writing more than one hundred years after the wars ended. He gave the longest and most complete account of the war with Hannibal. Ten books in his *History of Rome* are devoted to the seventeen years of the Second Punic War. These volumes were well-preserved. They have been passed down to modern times.

Livy's writing is filled with facts. It also includes speeches by the main characters. These quotes claim to be an exact record of what was said at the time. They are more likely to have been made up by the author. He wanted to show the true character of Hannibal and others who took part in the wars.[7]

Polybius' account is considered the best reference. Unfortunately, there are pieces missing. His record of Hannibal's story ends in 216 B.C. From that time on, researchers must depend on Livy's works.

Modern historians and writers use the works of these two authors. The texts are not firsthand accounts of Hannibal, but nothing else exists. Others who have written books about Hannibal rely on the two ancient authors. They hope the facts are accurate.

THE GREEK AUTHOR POLYBIUS

Polybius was born near the end of the third century B.C. The exact date is unknown. He was the son of a rich landowner. His home was in the mountains of Arcadia. Polybius learned to ride and to hunt. He served with the army in Greece. After he moved to Rome, he became a friend of the Scipio family. Polybius traveled. He was also a good observer of events that happened during his lifetime. He died at the age of eighty-two when he fell from his horse.

THE ROMAN AUTHOR LIVY

Livy was born at Patavium in 59 B.C. He moved to Rome
when he was about thirty years old. That was when he
started his lengthy history. Livy worked on *The History of
Rome* for over forty years. He wrote 142 volumes. Today,
35 still exist. His work ended with his death in 17 A.D.
Little additional information is known about his life.

The histories of Livy and Polybius have both been
translated. They can be read today. Livy was translated
into French, Italian, Spanish, and German. This
happened in middle of the sixteenth century. An English
version came later.

HANNIBAL'S INFLUENCE ON THE ROMAN EMPIRE

Hannibal and his wars shaped Roman civilization. He
wanted to stop Rome from ruling Carthage. If he had
succeeded, Hannibal would also have kept Rome from
ruling more territory around the Mediterranean. Some
suggest even greater consequences. If he had defeated
Rome, Hannibal would have changed the history of the
western world. Carthage might exist today, not Rome.

Hannibal is praised for his skills in warfare. He was
raised to fight. He traveled to Spain with his father's
army at age nine. He mastered the qualities of a great
general. His strategies were designed for each battle and

foe. He controlled the movements of warriors skillfully. He had a quick mind. He adapted easily to new situations.

For Hannibal every battlefield was a new opportunity.[8] He made the land work in his favor. He used the hills, valleys, bushes, and trees. Hannibal's officers were experienced soldiers. Fighting was their job. He selected the best riders and horses. He used all his resources to help him win. He proved he could beat enemies who had him outnumbered. For these reasons, he defeated the Roman legions time and time again.

Rome learned quickly from its defeats during the Punic wars. The Carthaginian fleet destroyed Rome's navy several times in the first war. Rome built vessels like those used by its foe. The Romans trained sailors to fight at close quarters. They learned from Carthaginian tactics. Then they added clever tactics of their own. By

ROME LEFT UNTOUCHED

At least twice during his years in Italy, Hannibal could have marched on Rome and ransacked it. Each time he decided not to. This is amazing since the city was always his goal. The commander of the Carthaginian cavalry offered this explanation. He said that Hannibal knew how to win victory but not how to use it.[9] In other words, he felt Hannibal understood what was needed to defeat his enemy in a battle. He did not think the general realized that people feared him most right after he won. That was the best time to strike Rome. The citizen's fears gave Hannibal the advantage.

the end of the Second Punic War, Rome's navy was the better fighting force.

The Second Punic War changed the Roman army. Until 216 B.C., it was manned by citizen recruits, who signed on to fight, but expected to go back to their farms when their service ended. The Romans used very basic tactics. When they prepared for battle, the soldiers stood side-by-side. They stretched out across the battlefield. All of them marched into battle at the same time. The basic theory was that the larger force could drive back a smaller one.

Roman generals eventually learned better strategies. They filled their legions with experienced soldiers. They became a well-trained force. Then they used all the manpower Rome, Italy, and their provinces could provide to fight Hannibal.

Publius Cornelius Scipio was the first Roman consul to master Hannibal's tactics.[10] He studied the general's battle formations. He made note of his favorite tricks. Scipio used those strategies and others he came up with on his own. He faced the Carthaginians with confidence.

Most of Scipio's legions at Zama were experienced soldiers. He depended on the help of skilled allies. He recruited cavalry support from the best in the world, the Numidians. He picked the time and place to fight his enemy. He used tactics and terrain carefully. With these lessons well learned, Scipio finally defeated Rome's number one enemy, Hannibal.

The Roman Empire, Hannibal, and the World Today

Rome's victory over Carthage changed the world. It destroyed the African city-state and ended its influence on civilization. From that time on, Roman culture spread throughout the countries and territories under its control. Carthaginian customs were forgotten. The Roman Empire built governments, made laws, shaped the architecture, and became the greatest power in the ancient world.

Rome conquered more lands. The Romans expanded their empire. It stretched into Europe. They claimed parts of North Africa and the Middle East. They maintained that empire for the next eight centuries.[11]

Rome left its mark on the world. It has lasted through time. Its influence exists even today in Western

These Roman ruins are in present-day Tunisia, very close to the former site of Carthage.

Europe and also in America.[12] Europeans settled in lands in the Western Hemisphere. They spread Latin-based languages. They brought systems of government developed by the Romans. They spread that culture throughout the New World. If Hannibal had defeated Rome after marching across the Alps none of this might have come to pass.

Carthage ceased to exist, but Hannibal's story did not die with it. Since the days of Polybius, historians have tried to follow the general's tracks from Spain, across southern Gaul, and into Italy. His tale lives on, even though we cannot be sure of all the facts.

It is certain that in 218 B.C., Hannibal Barca marched across the Alps with an army of foot soldiers, cavalry, and some forty elephants. He reached Italy with his huge force. Then Hannibal spent the next fifteen years trying to conquer his greatest enemy, Rome, a feat he was almost able to achieve.

CHRONOLOGY

264 B.C.—First Punic War begins.

247 B.C.—Hamilcar Barca takes command of the Carthaginian Army in Sicily; his son Hannibal Barca is born.

237 B.C.—Hamilcar and his army go to Spain; nine-year-old Hannibal accompanies him.

230 B.C.—Hamilcar dies; Hasdrubal, his son-in-law, takes command of the army in Spain.

221 B.C.—Hasdrubal is murdered; Hannibal becomes commander-in-chief of the Carthaginian army.

219 B.C.—Hannibal captures Saguntum.

218 B.C.—Rome declares war on Carthage; Hannibal marches from Spain and crosses the Alps into Italy. He defeats the Roman consul Scipio in the first major battle of the Second Punic War.

217 B.C.—Hannibal wins the Battle of Lake Trasimene.

216 B.C.—Hannibal wins another victory in the Battle of Cannae; the town of Capua negotiates a pact with Hannibal.

214 B.C.—Hannibal captures Tarentum in Italy;
–213 B.C. Romans recapture Saguntum in Spain.

211 B.C.—Hannibal marches on Rome; Capua surrenders to Rome; Publius Scipio is elected consul and takes his legions to Spain.

210 B.C.—Scipio takes New Carthage, the Carthaginian capital in Spain.

209 B.C.—Scipio defeats Hasdrubal Barca in Spain; Hasdrubal retreats to southern Gaul.

207 B.C.—Hasdrubal crosses the Alps to join Hannibal in Italy; Hasdrubal's army is defeated, and he is killed and beheaded.

206 B.C.—Carthaginian resistance in Spain ends.

204 B.C.—Scipio crosses to Africa with his legions.

203 B.C.—The Romans burn the Carthaginian army camp; Carthaginian envoys ask for peace terms; Mago is defeated in Italy; Hannibal and Mago are recalled to Carthage; Hannibal leaves Italy; Carthage breaks the peace agreement.

202 B.C.—Scipio and Hannibal meet; Carthage is defeated in the Battle of Zama, bringing the Second Punic War to an end.

201 B.C.—Peace agreement between Carthage and Rome is signed; Hannibal becomes chief magistrate of Carthage.

197 B.C.—Rome accuses Hannibal of helping an enemy of the state and demands his surrender. Hannibal escapes from Carthage and lives the rest of his life in exile.

183 B.C.—Hannibal drinks poison and dies at the age of sixty-four.

151 B.C.—Carthage declares war on Masinissa, breaking the peace agreement signed in 201 B.C.

150 B.C.—Rome declares war on Carthage, beginning the Third Punic War.

149 B.C.—Romans invade Africa.

146 B.C.—The Third Punic War ends with the capture and destruction of Carthage by the Roman commander Scipio Aemilianus.

CHAPTER NOTES

CHAPTER 1. ACROSS THE ALPS

1. Mark Healy, *Hannibal Smashes Rome's Army* (London: Osprey, 1994), p. 13.

2. Adrian Goldsworthy, *The Punic Wars* (London: Cassell & Co, 2000), p. 166.

3. Ernle Bradford, *Hannibal* (London: Folio Society, 1998), xiv.

4. Goldsworthy, p. 128.

5. Livy, *The War with Hannibal,* trans. Aubrey de Sélincourt, (Baltimore: Penguin Books, 1972), p. 58.

6. Ibid., p. 59.

7. Bradford, p. 36.

8. Livy, p. 60.

9. Ibid.

10. Ibid.

11. Goldsworthy, p. 166.

12. Bradford, p. 35.

13. John Peddie, *Hannibal's War* (Thrupp: Sutton Publishing Limited, 1997), p. 26.

14. Livy, p. 166.

15. Ibid., p. 63.

Chapter 2. Hannibal's Early Years

1. Ernle Bradford, *Hannibal* (London: Folio Society, 1998), p. 1.

2. Ibid., p. 5.

3. Adrian Goldsworthy, *The Punic Wars* (London: Cassell & Co, 2000), p. 95.

4. Bradford, p. 7.

5. "Battle of the Aegates (Egadi) Islands, 241 BC," *Hannibal Barca and the Punic Wars*, n.d., <http://www.barca.fsnet.co.uk/aegates.htm> (August 27, 2004).

6. Goldsworthy, p. 12.

7. Mark Healy, *Hannibal Smashes Rome's Army* (London: Osprey, 1994), p. 7.

8. Ibid.

9. Sir Gavin de Beer, *Hannibal: Challenging Rome's Supremacy* (New York: Viking Press, 1969), p. 95.

10. Livy, *The War with Hannibal*, trans. Aubrey de Sélincourt, (Baltimore: Penguin Books, 1965), p. 23.

11. Ibid., p. 96.

12. Ibid., p. 97.

13. Ibid., p. 24.

14. Ibid., p. 26.

15. Bradford, pp. 19–21.

16. Livy, p. 26.

Chapter 3. Hannibal In Command

1. Ernle Bradford, *Hannibal* (London: Folio Society, 1998), p. 20.

2. Ibid., p. 25.

3. Ibid., p. 36.

4. Polybius, *Rise of the Roman Empire* (London: Penguin Books, 1979), p. 191.

5. Bradford, p. 22.

6. John Peddie, *Hannibal's War* (Thrupp: Sutton Publishing Limited, 1997), p. 10.

7. Polybius, p. 192.

8. Mark Healy, *Hannibal Smashes Rome's Army* (London: Osprey, 1994), p. 9.

9. Peddie, p. 10.

10. Healy, p. 9.

11. Livy, *The War with Hannibal,* trans. Aubrey de Sélincourt, (Baltimore: Penguin Books, 1965), p. 44.

12. Adrian Goldsworthy, *The Punic Wars* (London: Cassell & Co., 2000), p. 153.

13. Livy, p. 46.

14. Bradford, p. 32.

15. Livy, p. 33.

CHAPTER 4. THE MARCH TO ITALY BEGINS

1. Livy, *The War with Hannibal,* trans. Aubrey de Sélincourt, (Baltimore: Penguin Books, 1965), p. 46.

2. John Peddie, *Hannibal's War* (Thrupp: Sutton Publishing Limited, 1997), p. 14.

3. Ernle Bradford, *Hannibal* (London: Folio Society, 1998), p. 33.

4. Livy, p. 47.

5. Polybius, *Rise of the Roman Empire* (London: Penguin Books, 1979), p. 212.

6. Adrian Goldsworthy, *The Punic Wars* (London: Cassell & Co., 2000), p. 159.

7. Livy, p. 47.

8. Ibid., p. 50.

9. Ibid.

10. Sir Gavin de Beer, *Hannibal: Challenging Rome's Supremacy* (New York: Viking Press, 1969), p. 127.

11. Livy, p. 51.

12. Ibid.

CHAPTER 5. ROME PREPARES FOR WAR

1. Polybius, *Rise of the Roman Empire* (London: Penguin Books, 1979), p. 197.

2. Ibid., p. 215.

3. Ibid., p. 222.

4. Livy, *The War with Hannibal,* trans. Aubrey de Sélincourt, (Baltimore: Penguin Books, 1965), p. 53.

5. Ibid., pp. 53–54.

6. Ibid.

7. Polybius, p. 218.

8. Adrian Goldsworthy, *The Punic Wars* (London: Cassell & Co, 2000), p. 163.

9. Ibid.

10. Ibid., p. 163.

CHAPTER 6. HANNIBAL ROUTS THE ROMANS

1. Polybius, *Rise of the Roman Empire* (London: Penguin Books, 1979), p. 231.

2. John Peddie, *Hannibal's War* (Thrupp: Sutton Publishing Limited, 1997), p. 31.

3. Polybius, p. 233.

4. Livy, *The War with Hannibal,* trans. Aubrey de Sélincourt, (Baltimore: Penguin Books, 1965), p. 72.

5. Ibid., p. 73.

6. Polybius, *Rise of the Roman Empire* (London: Penguin Books, 1979), p. 235.

7. Livy, p. 74.

8. Ibid., p. 77.

9. Ibid., p. 78.

10. Ibid.

11. Ibid., p. 80.

12. Ibid., p. 81.

13. Ibid., p. 82.

14. Ibid., p. 83.

15. Sir Gavin de Beer, *Hannibal: Challenging Rome's Supremacy* (New York: Viking Press, 1969), p. 188.

16. Ibid., p. 189.

CHAPTER 7. ANOTHER VICTORIOUS SEASON

1. Ernle Bradford, *Hannibal* (London: Folio Society, 1998), p. 85.

2. Polybius, *Rise of the Roman Empire* (London: Penguin Books, 1979), p. 247.

3. Ibid.

4. Bradford, p. 86.

5. Livy, *The War with Hannibal*, trans. Aubrey de Sélincourt, (Baltimore: Penguin Books, 1965), p. 101.

6. Bradford, p. 92.

7. Ibid., p. 94.

8. Ibid., p. 96.

9. Livy, p. 111.

10. Ibid., p. 114.

11. Ibid., p 120.

12. Bradford, p. 96.

13. Polybius, p. 264

CHAPTER 8. THE BATTLE OF CANNAE

1. Ernle Bradford, *Hannibal* (London: Folio Society, 1998), p. 110.

2. Mark Healy, *Hannibal Smashes Rome's Army* (London: Osprey, 1994), p. 69.

3. Livy, *The War with Hannibal,* trans. Aubrey de Sélincourt, (Baltimore: Penguin Books, 1965), p. 141.

4. Ibid.

5. Ibid., p. 145.

6. Ibid.

7. Ibid., p. 148.

8. Ibid.

9. Ibid., p. 151.

10. Sir Gavin de Beer, *Hannibal: Challenging Rome's Supremacy* (New York: Viking Press, 1969), p. 221.

CHAPTER 9. WAR IN ITALY AND ABROAD

1. Livy, *The War with Hannibal,* trans. Aubrey de Sélincourt, (Baltimore: Penguin Books, 1965), p. 209.

2. John Peddie, *Hannibal's War* (Thrupp: Sutton Publishing Limited, 1997), p. 111.

3. Ibid., p. 116.

4. Ibid., p. 139.

5. Ibid., p. 140.

6. Sir Gavin de Beer, *Hannibal: Challenging Rome's Supremacy* (New York: Viking Press, 1969), p. 236.

7. Peddie, p. 142.

8. De Beer, p. 248.

CHAPTER 10. CARTHAGE LOSES GROUND

1. John Peddie, *Hannibal's War* (Thrupp: Sutton Publishing Limited, 1997), p. 165.

2. Ibid., pp. 167–168.

3. Livy, *The War with Hannibal*, trans. Aubrey de Sélincourt, (Baltimore: Penguin Books, 1965), p. 442.

4. Livy, p. 449.

5. Peddie, p. 175.

6. Sir Gavin de Beer, *Hannibal: Challenging Rome's Supremacy* (New York: Viking Press, 1969), p. 260.

7. Peddie, p. 179.

8. Livy, p. 496.

9. Peddie, p. 182.

CHAPTER 11. CARTHAGE'S LAST BATTLES IN EUROPE

1. Livy, *The War with Hannibal*, trans. Aubrey de Sélincourt, (Baltimore: Penguin Books, 1965), p. 513.

2. Ibid., p. 515.

3. Ibid.

4. John Peddie, *Hannibal's War* (Thrupp: Sutton Publishing Limited, 1997), p. 183.

5. Ibid.

6. Ibid., p. 185.

7. Ibid., p. 187.

8. Livy, p. 644.

9. Sir Gavin de Beer, *Hannibal: Challenging Rome's Supremacy* (New York: Viking Press, 1969), p. 284.

CHAPTER 12. WAR IN AFRICA

1. Polybius, *Rise of the Roman Empire* (London: Penguin Books, 1979), p. 464.

2. Ibid., pp. 465–466.

3. John Peddie, *Hannibal's War* (Thrupp: Sutton Publishing Limited, 1997), p. 201.

4. Polybius, p. 469.

5. Ibid., pp. 469–470.

6. Ibid., p. 472.

7. Livy, *The War with Hannibal,* trans. Aubrey de Sélincourt, (Baltimore: Penguin Books, 1965), p. 661.

8. De Beer, p. 290.

9. Polybius, p. 481.

10. Ibid.

CHAPTER 13. HANNIBAL'S LAST YEARS

1. Livy, *The War with Hannibal,* trans. Aubrey de Sélincourt, (Baltimore: Penguin Books, 1965), p. 675.

2. John Peddie, *Hannibal's War* (Thrupp: Sutton Publishing Limited, 1997), p. 230.

3. Ibid.

4. Ernle Bradford, *Hannibal* (London: Folio Society, 1998), p. 231.

5. Sir Gavin de Beer, *Hannibal: Challenging Rome's Supremacy* (New York: Viking Press, 1969), p. 296.

6. Bradford, p. 233.

7. De Beer, p. 297.

8. Michael O. Akinde, "Publius Cornelius Scipio Africanus (236-184): Final Act," *Fenrir.dk,* © 2003,

<http://www.fenrir.dk/history/bios/scipio/finalact.php> (November 6, 2004).

   9. De Beer, p. 297.

   10. Ibid., p. 299.

   11. Ibid.

   12. Ibid.

   13. Peddie, p. 203.

   14. De Beer, p. 300.

CHAPTER 14. THE THIRD PUNIC WAR

   1. T. A. Dorey and D. R. Dudley, *Rome Against Carthage* (New York: Doubleday & Company, Inc., 1972), p. 155.

   2. Ibid., p. 157.

   3. "Third Punic War," Wikipedia, the free encyclopedia, <http://en.wipedoa.org/wiki/Third_Punic_War> (November 8, 2004).

   4. Dorey and Dudley, p. 161.

   5. Ibid.

   6. Ibid., p. 162.

   7. Ibid., p. 169.

   8. Ibid., p. 171.

   9. "Third Punic War 149–146 BC," *Hannibal Barca and the Punic Wars*, n.d., <http://www.barca.fsnet.co.uk/punic3.htm> (November 8, 2004).

   10. Paul Halsall, "Ancient History Sourcebook: Polybius: The Third Punic War, 149-164 B.C.," *Ancient History Sourcebook*, July 1998, <http://fordham.edu/halsall/ancient/polybius-punic3.html> (November 8, 2004).

   11. "Third Punic War."

CHAPTER 15. CARTHAGE YIELDS TO ROME

1. Ernle Bradford, *Hannibal* (London: Folio Society, 1998), xiii.

2. Mark Healy, *Hannibal Smashes Rome's Army* (London: Osprey, 1994), p. 94.

3. T.A. Dorey and D. R. Dudley, *Rome Against Carthage* (New York: Doubleday & Company, Inc., 1972.), xiii.

4. Adrian Goldsworthy, *The Punic Wars* (London: Cassell & Co, 2000), p. 15.

5. Bradford, xiv.

6. Ibid.

7. Ibid.

8. Ibid., p. 239.

9. Ibid., xiii.

10. Ibid., p. 239.

11. Bradford, xiii.

12. Goldsworthy, p. 13.

Glossary

ALLY—A country or group that joins with another for a common purpose such as war.

CITADEL—A fortress, often built on a high point, for defense of a city.

CONSUL—Highest-ranking official of the ancient Roman republic.

ENVOY—A diplomatic messenger sent by a government.

FORAGE—To get or take food and provisions.

FORTIFICATION—A fort or defensive earthworks or wall.

GALLEY—A single-decked ship propelled by oars and sails.

GARRISON—A fortified place with troops and guns.

HARRY—To pillage and plunder or raid repeatedly.

JAVELIN—A light spear for throwing.

LANCE—A long wooden shaft with a sharp spearhead used as a thrusting weapon.

LAY SIEGE—To mount a prolonged blockade or assault on a city or fortress.

LEGION—A military division of several thousand Roman troops.

MERCENARY—A soldier paid to fight in a foreign army.

MISSILE—Something launched or shot during a battle, like a stone or an arrow.

MOLE—A barrier of stone built in a body of water.

PALISADE—A fence used for fortification or defense.

PIKESMAN—A warrior armed with a spear.

PUNIC—A term for ancient Carthage or its people.

SENATE—The Carthaginian governing body, similar to the Roman Senate.

SLINGER—A man using a sling to throw missiles in ancient warfare.

TRIBUNAL—A court of justice.

WEAPONS STORE—A place armies keep armor, weapons, and ammunition.

FURTHER READING

Green, Robert. *Hannibal* (First Book). Minneapolis, Minn.: Sagebrush, 1999.

Henty, G. A. *The Young Carthaginian: A Story of the Times of Hannibal*. Lake Wales, Fla.: Lost Classics Book Co., 2001.

Nardo, Don. *Battle of Zama: Battles of the Ancient World*. San Diego, Calif.: Lucent Books, 1996.

———. *The Punic Wars*. San Diego: Lucent Books, 1996.

———. *The Roman Army: An Instrument of Power*. San Diego: Lucent Books, 2004.

Steele, Philip. *Ancient Rome: History in Stone*. Berkeley, Calif.: Silver Dolphin, 2002.

INTERNET ADDRESSES

HISTORY FOR KIDS: FIRST PUNIC WAR
<http://www.historyforkids.org/learn/romans/history/
punicwars.htm>

HISTORY FOR KIDS: SECOND PUNIC WAR
<http://www.historyforkids.org/learn/romans/history/
secondpunic.htm>

**SOCIAL STUDIES FOR KIDS, HANNIBAL: ANCIENT
ROME'S GREATEST ENEMY**
<http://www.socialstudiesforkids.com/articles/
worldhistory/hannibal1.htm>

INDEX